Global Christian Library Series

The Holy Spirit

**This book
belongs to:
*Jeremey Mullin***

Langham
GLOBAL LIBRARY

The Holy Spirit

Lord and Life-Giver

Ivan Satyavrata

Series Editor: David Smith
Consulting Editor: Joe Kapolyo

© Ivan Satyavrata, 2009

Published 2012 by Langham Global Library
an imprint of Langham Creative Projects

Langham Partnership
PO Box 296, Carlisle, Cumbria, CA3 9WZ, UK
www.langham.org

ISBNs:
978-1-907713-08-8   print
978-1-907713-21-7   Mobi
978-1-907713-22-4   ePub

First published 2009 by Inter-Varsity Press, ISBN: 978-1-84474-351-3
This edition 2012 by Langham Global Library

British Library Cataloguing-in-Publication Data
Satyavrata, Ivan.
  The Holy Spirit : lord and life-giver.
  1. Holy Spirit.
  I. Title
  231.3-dc23

  ISBN-13: 9781907713088

Cover & typesetting: projectluz.com

CONTENTS

*'We believe . . . in the Holy Spirit,
the Lord and the Life-giver . . .'*
                              The Apostles' Creed

*For Sheila, Rahul and Rohan
God's precious gifts . . . my pride and joy!*

SERIES PREFACE

This book forms part of *The Global Christian Library* series published by Langham Literature, a subdivision of the Langham Partnership International.

The twentieth century saw a dramatic shift in the Christian centre of gravity. There are now many more Christians in Africa, Asia and Latin America than there are in Europe and North America. Two major issues have resulted, both of which *The Global Christian Library* seeks to address.

First, the basic theological texts available to pastors, students and lay readers in the Majority World (sometimes referred to as the Developing World) have for too long been written by Western authors from a Western perspective. There is now a need for more books by non-Western writers that reflect their own cultures. In consequence, *The Global Christian Library* includes work by gifted writers from the developing world who are resolved to be both biblically faithful and contextually relevant.

Second, Western readers need to be able to benefit from the wisdom and insight of our sisters and brothers in other parts of the world. Given the decay of many Western churches, we urgently need an injection of non-Western Christian vitality.

The adjective 'global' in the title of this seres reflects our desire that biblical understanding will flow freely in all directions. We pray that *The Global Christian Library* will open up channels of communication, in fulfilment of the Apostle Paul's conviction that it is only *together with all the Lord's people* that we will be able to grasp the dimensions of Christ's love (Ephesians 3:18).

Never before in the church's long history has this possibility been so close to realization. We hope and pray that *The Global Christian Library* may play a part in making it a reality in the twenty-first century.

Joe M. Kapolyo
David W. Smith

PREFACE

It is impossible to love God and also be dispassionate about the *study* of God. Deep devotion to Jesus and an all-consuming desire to see his glory fill the earth should fuel the passion of anyone who ventures to write about God and help illuminate other people's understanding of God and his ways. Few themes call for as much of a blending of mind and heart as that of the Holy Spirit. The spate of literature on the topic in recent years, while indicating growth in interest, also reflects sometimes divergent – often strongly disputed – perspectives on various aspects of the Holy Spirit's person and work.

The heat and dust generated by debate over some controversial questions has, however, frequently obscured essential underlying concurrence on more crucial issues among those with a shared commitment to the authority of Scripture. I am thankful to the Langham Partnership International and the editors of the Global Christian Library project for the opportunity to outline a biblical and theological basis for these common affirmations, while acknowledging with sensitivity real differences of interpretation on some matters among evangelicals around the globe.

My gratitude and appreciation to LPI extends beyond this writing project to John Stott's imaginative vision for strengthening the foundations of the church in the majority world by investing in the development of potential leaders from the non-Western world. As a participant and beneficiary of this project I am deeply grateful to Uncle John himself, Chris Wright, Merritt Sawyer and others within the LPI family for their faithful stewardship of this vision and strategic investment towards the cause of Christ in the majority world.

I am conscious of my indebtedness to a large community of family, friends and colleagues who have through the years helped shape my faith experience and life in Christ. While they are too many to list by name, this work reflects the cumulative influence of teachers, scholars and colleagues at Southern Asia Bible College, Bangalore; Union Biblical Seminary, Pune; Regent College, Vancouver, B. C.; and the Oxford Centre for Mission Studies, Oxford.

This book would not have reached its present form or have been successfully concluded without the wise and patient counsel of the editors, John Stott and David Smith. David has been a constant source of encouragement and pastoral support, especially during some difficult moments in the course of this project. I am grateful for the professionalism of Philip Duce and the staff at IVP, who have been both extremely thorough and immensely supportive in preparing the manuscript for publication. My wife, Sheila, and sons, Rahul and Rohan, have walked closely with me along this journey. As with everything else, I could never have made it without their support and encouragement.

I pray that this book will be a worthy tribute to the blessed Holy Spirit and his gracious workings. I pray that regardless of its shortcomings, it will help make the praise of our triune God more glorious!

Ivan Satyavrata

Kolkata, India, August 2008

1

The Wind Blows Where It Wills

The Spirit and Religious Experience

The train was due to arrive on the platform in five minutes. Although I was carrying study tapes, books and work with me, I was still not looking forward to the twenty-hour train journey ahead. It was really a thought rather than a prayer: *Lord, I really don't feel up to a debate or argument with anyone. It would be nice if during the train journey I could meet someone who was a genuine seeker – someone whom the Holy Spirit had already prepared.* Three hours later the conversation began.

Priya was a creative designer, probably in her early forties. Obviously well educated, she had lived abroad, was married to a successful corporate executive and was the mother of two boys. 'I am a teacher of theology' was my polite answer to what appeared to be a casual social query, and was surprised by the response. Her face lit up and she moved a seat closer: 'I am interested in knowing how I can have a deeper experience with God. I am a seeker – can you tell me more?'

I spent the best part of the next four hours listening and sharing as the lady described various experiments in her journey within contemporary Hinduism, and I shared how my own search for truth and meaning in life had been fulfilled in Christ. Halfway through our conversation a quiet young man who had been paying close attention to our conversation began to express deep interest. He was also a sincere seeker on his way to visit a famous guru whom he believed would guide him to spiritual enlightenment. To my astonishment, later in the evening, two middle-aged couples in the adjoining compartment, fellow-travellers who had been listening to our conversation, also began to participate in the discussion. They were on their way back after having just concluded a religious pilgrimage to several temples in the south. The evening ended with our exchanging visiting cards and my praying with Priya: for her mother who was dying of cancer, for the difficulties in her family situation and for the living Christ to fill the God-shaped vacuum her life.

This experience was a forceful reminder to me of what is undoubtedly the most critical question of our times: *Can I have a genuine experience of God in the here and now?* In most parts of the non-Western world, people have always been at home with the notion of religious experience. Thus the vast majority of cultures outside Europe and North America have always viewed nonphysical realities as having real existence. These cultures include followers of the primal religions found in Africa, Asia, Latin America and other parts of the world, as well as Hindus, Muslims, Buddhists and devotees of other Eastern religions. They routinely accept the reality of the spirit world and accordingly view people as having the capacity for two kinds of experience, one, of the physical world, and the other, of the non-physical world, both of which exert a powerful influence on human life.

The post-Enlightenment West, on the other hand, for the most part, has relegated this dimension to the realm of poetic imagination or the pre-modern world of superstition, along with fairies, genies and ghosts. This modern attitude of scepticism towards the non-physical and the supernatural has its roots in the seventeenth-century Enlightenment project's quest for certainty in knowledge and its conviction that true knowledge is obtained only through sense experience. The Enlightenment thus led humanity into a space-time box, programmed by the laws of natural science within which there was no room for a genuine experience of divine-human encounter. Under the Enlightenment influence a liberal and critical Christian tradition developed, which nurtured an intellectual scepticism towards miraculous elements in the Bible and virtually denied the possibility of a direct experience with divine reality.

The latter half of the twentieth century, however, witnessed the abandonment of many of the intellectual assumptions of the Enlightenment. Many discoveries of physical science, anthropology, biology, psychology and medicine split open the space-time box of the Enlightenment mindset, opening up the possibility of a divine-human encounter beyond the realm of sense experience (Kelsey 1972: 15–140). And several global indications signalled the waning influence of the Enlightenment world view.

The first wind that blew across the West was a widespread disillusionment with the modern dream reflected in the counterculture movement of the mid-twentieth century. This movement was motivated by a rejection of the preceding generation's obsession with materialism and was marked by an intense quest for spiritual reality. Large numbers of Western youth turned to Eastern religions and the mystical spirituality offered by gurus and god men in order to fill this spiritual void. Others turned to spiritualism, the occult, the revival of pre-Christian nature religion and the emergence of New Age spirituality.

The universal discontent with humanistic materialism in the West had its counterpart in the dismissal of communistic materialism in Eastern Europe. The last quarter of the twentieth century thus witnessed a tumultuous wind of change in Eastern Europe with the collapse of confidence in Marxist utopian ideals. They were found wanting in their ability to satisfy the physical needs of the masses and just as bankrupt in their ability to respond meaningfully to the intimations of the transcendent in the human heart.

I had heard about and read this assessment at different times, but, following a visit to Kiev in the Ukraine in 2006, came away convinced. I was teaching a short course entitled *Christ, the Human Face of God* to a select group of bishops and Pentecostal leaders from Russia, Latvia, Siberia, Belarus and other parts of Eastern Europe and Central Asia. When we came to the topic 'Christ and Marxism', I thought it better to draw out their reflections on the issue rather than share my limited knowledge of the subject. There was striking concurrence among the rich responses I received, perhaps best summarized in the words of a professor of philosophy whose search had led her to explore various forms of Eastern mysticism, including some esoteric sects of Hinduism. She said simply, 'Marxism left a spiritual void in us that only Christ could satisfy!'

In the South and East, the years immediately following liberation from colonial captivity in the second half of the twentieth century were marked by a strong assertion of national identity and ethnic pride. This journey of self-discovery often included the recovery and revival of indigenous culture and religion, giving rise to another wind of change affecting the global spiritual climate. The rich and ancient traditions of mystical spirituality possessed by the traditional religions of Africa and Latin America and Eastern religions such as Buddhism and Hinduism experienced resurgence, and were often also exported to Europe and North America.

The signs were thus unmistakable. Materialistic modernity had run its course, and brought in its wake a surge of interest in spirituality, and a growing pervasive hunger for a genuine experience of God in the here and now. In their popular bestseller, published in 1990, *Megatrends 2000*, social forecasters Naisbitt and Aburdene detail clear signs of what they herald as a 'worldwide multidenominational religious revival' at the dawn of the third millennium. In discerning the changing spirit of the times, they observe, 'Scientists once thought that the search to find "truth" would bring a megatrend to worship of science instead of religion . . . [but] the powerful countertrend of the religious revival is repudiating blind faith in science and technology' (1990: 251).

The changing spirit of the times was clearly reflected among Christians in shifting attitudes to the role of the Holy Spirit in Christian experience and in the life of the church. At the tail end of the fourth century, one of the church's greatest thinkers, Augustine, lamented the neglect of the Holy Spirit in the following terms:

> Wise and spiritual men have written numerous books on the Father and the Son . . . On the contrary, the Holy Spirit has not yet been studied so extensively and with like care by the learned and famous commentators on the divine scriptures . . . (Quoted in McDonnell 1985: 191)

In the mid-twentieth century, the subject of the Holy Spirit was still being described as 'the last unexplored theological frontier' (Berdyaev 1946: 22). Not long after, Karl Barth anticipated the coming of a theology through the Holy Spirit,

> where the Holy Spirit would dominate and be decisive. Everything that one believes, reflects, and says about God the Father and God the Son . . . would be demonstrated and clarified basically through God the Holy Spirit . . . (Quoted in McDonnell 1985: 193)

Even while Barth was penning his profound prediction, winds of change had began to blow both within and outside the church.

The evangelical awakening of the eighteenth century, nurtured under the passionate preaching of Wesley and Whitefield, had already drawn renewed attention to the experiential dimension of biblical Christianity in reaction to the spiritual vacuousness of rationalistic deism. But by the second half of the twentieth century the church worldwide began to feel the impact of a stream of evangelicalism that grew into one of the most significant forces for the spread of the Christian faith in the twentieth century. The Pentecostal movement and the charismatic renewal that followed gave birth to a new expression of Christianity, which had a New Testament type of enthusiastic spirituality as its distinguishing characteristic. Huge numbers of people of all classes and cultures are involved in the related movements of Pentecostalism and, as a result, the scope of its influence on the shape of contemporary global Christianity has been phenomenal. While the movement has not been without its detractors, a significant majority of Christians in the world today either warmly embrace or remain cautiously open to its essential emphases while rejecting its excesses.

The second half of the twentieth century thus witnessed an unprecedented resurgence of interest in the doctrine of the Holy Spirit and spirituality. As Alistair McGrath observes:

> The rise of the charismatic movement within virtually every mainstream church has ensured that the Holy Spirit figures prominently on the theological agenda. A new experience of the reality and power of the Spirit has had a major impact upon the theological discussion of the person and work of the Holy Spirit. (McGrath 1994: 240)

Thus no longer can the Holy Spirit be called, in Gregory of Nazianzus' words, the *theos agraptos*, the 'God about whom no one writes' (quoted in Kärkkäinen 1998: 19). Nor can he be called 'the forgotten God' or the 'Cinderella' of the Trinity (McDonnell 2003: 2). The situation today is very different from the fourth century or even the early decades of the twentieth century, with a significant amount of attention given to the Holy Spirit in Christian devotional experience, church and mission practice, theological discussion and literary output (Kärkkäinen 1998: 20–21).

In his well-known discourse on the nature and importance of the new birth in John 3, Jesus uses the metaphor of the wind to illustrate to Nicodemus the mysterious and sovereign nature of the Holy Spirit's workings: 'The wind blows wherever it pleases. You hear its sound, but you cannot tell where it comes from or where it is going' (John 3:8). These words of Jesus offer much hope and promise to a generation that seeks reality beyond the world of cold logic, deductive reasoning and academic analysis. As a result, today we are witnessing an upsurge of various forms of spiritual experience throughout the world. But is this openness to the world of religious experience essentially healthy or harmful? What does the Bible have to say about religious experience?

The Old Testament faith is firmly grounded in a tradition of divine encounter as the basis of faith working itself out in obedience. The patriarchal faith of Abraham and his immediate descendants was clearly based on their experiences of divine encounter, and the patriarchs marked these significant moments in their lives by the altars they built. Moses' claim to greatness was based on his privilege of having communed with God face to face. The children of Israel received the law of God only after they had experienced the revelation of the awesome majesty of God at Mount Sinai. And from their experiences of the divine presence in multiple ways and circumstances the prophets derived their authority to speak.

When we turn to the New Testament, we find that the Christian faith rests fundamentally on the Christ-event. The faith is grounded in the historical facts concerning the birth, life, death and resurrection of Jesus, culminating in Pentecost, the early church's first experience of the Holy Spirit. While all of these aspects of the Christ-event are important and integrally related, in practice the church has often failed to emphasize adequately the significance of Pentecost. The testimony of the earliest disciples of Jesus was grounded in their eyewitness experience of the risen Lord and his personal commissioning of them. However, it was their lived-out experience of the Holy Spirit following Pentecost that gave spiritual power and authenticity to their witness (Acts 1:8).

Accordingly, the New Testament defines apostolic authority in terms of experiential knowledge derived from close association with the person of Jesus. Peter thus affirms that his testimony about Jesus was not a recounting of cleverly invented stories, but flowed from his experience as one of the 'eye-witnesses of his majesty' (2 Pet. 1:16). John likewise writes that his proclamation is based on what he has seen, heard and touched – his personal experience of the Word of life (1 John 1:1–3). Paul's teaching, too, assumes the reality of a personal experience of the Holy Spirit. The tenor of many of his references to the Spirit seem to make sense only when understood as alluding to a definite experience of the Spirit: 'For you did not receive a spirit that makes you a slave again to fear, but you received the Spirit of sonship. And by him we cry, "Abba, Father" ' (Rom. 8:15); 'Does God give you his Spirit and work miracles among you because you observe the law, or because you believe what you heard?' (Gal. 3:5).

Biblical Christianity is thus not totally discordant with the spirit of our times. On one hand, the abundance and variety of religious experience the Bible records offers legitimacy to the contemporary revival of interest in religious experience. However, not only does the Bible affirm the human quest for reality, but it also invites seekers to a life-transforming encounter with the living God through Jesus Christ. The present openness to the possibility of a direct experiential encounter with divine reality thus offers great potential for evangelism. To a generation that seeks desperately for a genuine experience of God, Christians can present Jesus Christ, who promises, 'I am the bread of life. He who comes to me will never go hungry, and he who believes in me will never be thirsty' (John 6:35).

This potential is, however, not without its dangers. The most obvious danger in the present emphasis on religious experience is the tendency to accord subjective experience final authority in matters of truth. I recall an occasion when, as a young believer, I met an acquaintance on my way home from a prayer meeting. The prayer meeting had been a wonderful emotional and spiritual experience, and, in witnessing to this person whom I knew was addicted to drugs, I described how the prayer meeting had made me feel joyful, loving and at peace with the world. He responded with a knowing and patronizing smile and, to my dismay, claimed to have a similar experience every time he had a 'fix'. Despite my desperate attempts to distinguish his experience from mine, he insisted that his experience was a true experience of God and welcomed me as a fellow-believer to the ranks of the enlightened. He walked away leaving me discouraged, confused and speechless.

This ultimate autonomy of experience, traditionally a characteristic of Hinduism and Eastern religions in general, has more recently become a distinguishing feature of New Age philosophy, some forms of liberal theology, postmodernity and some Pentecostal sects as well. The fact of the matter is that every religious experience is not necessarily an authentic experience of God. There must be some basis for a discernment of spirits that distinguishes between a religious experience effected by human sin or demonic influence and an authentic encounter with the divine. Christians believe the Bible provides this external authoritative basis for judging between true and false religious experience.

Thus, as precious as his experience of the Holy Spirit is to him, a Christian must allow the Bible to judge his experience. Jesus did say that 'The wind blows wherever it pleases' (John 3:8) but also stated what the mandate of the Spirit would be: 'When the Counsellor comes, whom I will send from the Father, the Spirit of truth who goes out from the Father, he will testify about me . . . He will bring glory to me . . .' (John 15:26; 16:14). A true experience of the Spirit must conform to the biblical testimony concerning Christ and be consistent with the teaching of Scripture. Most Christians recognize the sovereign hand of God in the contemporary recovery of emphasis on the Holy Spirit's person and work. But, while there is much to celebrate in this focus on the Spirit and his workings after several centuries of relative neglect, there is a pressing need to relate our present experience of the Spirit to the teaching of God's Word. This is a task to which the rest of this book is devoted.

Perhaps the most pressing issue implicit in Jesus' description of the Spirit's sovereign activity, and of critical significance in today's context of growing cultural and religious plurality, is recognizing where and how the Holy Spirit is present and at work today. Since most religions have some view of 'spirit', why not discard the cumbersome Christian doctrine of the Trinity and explore theological continuity based on Spirit? How is the Holy Spirit different from the Spirit or spirits in other religions? Another set of critical theological questions arises in relation to the Spirit's identity. In the light of Jesus' description of the Holy Spirit as 'wind' (elsewhere 'breath', 'water' or 'fire'), are we to conceive of the Spirit more properly as a *force* or a *person*? And, as a corollary, *What is the Spirit's relation to the Father and to Jesus?*

A host of other questions of critical pastoral and devotional significance come to mind:

- Does every Christian have the Spirit or is the Spirit meant only for the super-saints?
- Do I need to speak in tongues to prove I am a follower of Jesus?
- Is there any difference between the present-day exercise of the gift of prophecy and the New Age practice of 'channelling'?
- Am I being fanatical if I ask God to heal me today when I am sick?

Sincere, Bible-believing Christians offer a variety of answers to questions of this nature, often a source of confusion and controversy. This book is meant to provide an introductory biblical understanding of these and other related issues for Christians whose hearts are wide open to the wind of the Holy Spirit, but who sincerely desire to exercise a biblically informed gift of discernment.

2

The Spirit and the Church

The Spirit in the Life of the Church

It would have been wonderful if Jesus had lived in the twentieth century when his legacy could have been captured for posterity in some form of audio, video or digital recording. It would have been very helpful if he had at least himself written out a scroll or manifesto that clearly laid out his self-understanding, outlined his teachings and spelled out his mission. Jesus did not, however, choose to do that. All Jesus left behind when he left this world was wrapped up in the experience of the earliest Christian community – the first disciples' memory of and testimony to the Christ-event.

While on earth, Jesus had promised, 'But the Counsellor, the Holy Spirit, whom the Father will send in my name, will teach you all things and will remind you of everything I have said to you . . . when he, the Spirit of truth, comes, he will guide you into all truth' (John 14:26; 16:13). It was their experience of the Holy Spirit that gave the testimony of the earliest Christian community authenticity and vitality. The New Testament church was born with the coming of the Holy Spirit upon the earliest disciples of Jesus on the day of Pentecost. Since then, the church's experience of the Holy Spirit corporately and individually marks it as the locus of God's own personal presence. The evidence of the Spirit's presence in the life of the church is what sets God's people apart from all other people on earth.

But what does this mean and how is this reflected in the life of the church today? Has the Holy Spirit been effectively domesticated so that he works only through church structures, institutions and sacraments? Or do these in fact stifle the Spirit's freedom, so that he works apart from or sometimes even in opposition to the organized church? The twentieth century has witnessed the outbreak and emergence of a number of Spirit-led revival movements. The phenomenon of revival, crucial to the life of the church, is the inevitable reaction to the coldness of ritual and formality that frequently creeps in. The Holy Spirit is not, however, a modern invention of the church, nor did the Father suddenly decide as an afterthought to send him to the twentieth-century church. Our excitement at what we observe God doing in and through these movements must not blind us to the work of the Spirit in the life of the church through the centuries.

A leading Indian Christian thinker of the previous generation made this somewhat provocative observation: 'When the Holy Spirit became a distant reality and then a dogma, when Jesus went to heaven and did not return, we thought of a Church and built one' (Chenchiah 1939: 96). Not many who take the biblical testimony seriously would give much credence to this blunt and radical statement, but it reflects an underlying impulse that is perhaps more widely prevalent. Thus many enthusiastic Christians today are sincerely convinced that the organized church is indeed a hindrance to the free movement of the Spirit, that the Holy Spirit cannot work within obsolete church structures and hence is more at work outside than within the church. This tension between organization and movement, ritual and charismata, form and freedom (in other words, church and Spirit) is not, however, unique to our modern experience. It has been intrinsic to the growth and development of the Christian movement since its inception.

While some church people may find it diffcult to believe that there can be a genuine work of the Holy Spirit outside the structures of the organized church, we sometimes encounter radical enthusiasts who remain convinced that church organization and form restrict the free activity of the Holy Spirit. Do sincere followers of Christ really have to make a choice between belonging to the church or following the leading of the Spirit? In this chapter we explore the church's experience of the Spirit prior to the modern period for some light on this issue. We do this in full realization of the fact that our understanding of the Holy Spirit will never be complete if we do not take into consideration two thousand years of the Spirit's presence and activity in the life of the church.

The church fathers

The Acts of the Apostles portrays the earliest church as living with an immediate awareness of the presence and power of the Holy Spirit. The Spirit was active in the life of the church, inspiring prophecy, manifesting charismatic gifts and empowering the church's apostolic witness. In summarizing the impact of the Holy Spirit upon the first-century church, Billy Graham observes:

> They had no Bibles, no seminaries, nor Bible schools. No radios or telephones. No printing presses. No churches. Nothing! However, they turned the world upside down in one generation. What did they have? They had an experience with the living Christ. They had the filling of the Holy Spirit. (Quoted in Durasoff 1972: 30)

This rhetorical assertion obviously does not call into question the centrality of the Bible to Christian faith any more than it minimizes the value of theological reflection, ministerial training or the employment of technology in the service of the church's mission. But it does challenge the modern church to follow the New Testament believing community's example of total dependence on the Holy Spirit's empowering presence.

On the other hand, we sometimes tend to idealize the first-century church, as if the earliest Christian community's immediate experience of the Spirit somehow exempted them from the human struggles that plague the church today. Nothing could be further from the truth. As John Stott reminds us:

> There is a danger lest we romanticize the early church, speaking of it with bated breath as if it had no blemishes. For then we shall miss the rivalries, hypocrisies, immoralities and heresies which troubled the church then as now. Nevertheless, one thing is certain. Christ's church had been overwhelmed by the Holy Spirit, who thrust it out to witness. (Stott 1990: 10)

Every student of the New Testament knows that most of the epistles were written in the heat of doctrinal controversy or ecclesiastical malpractice. A striking illustration is Paul's first letter to the Corinthians, written against the backdrop of excesses in the early church's experience of the Spirit, particularly in the misuse of the charismatic gifts. Thus even in the early formative stages of the Christian faith, we observe a tension between freedom and form – life in the Spirit and spiritual authority in the life of the church. We see this tension persist in the life of the church in subsequent eras.

The church fathers were key spokesmen of the Christian faith who recorded the first four centuries of its development. Their testimony is important due to their proximity to the apostolic era and also because they represent a period of united Christian witness prior to the church's division into Eastern and Western streams. The Spirit's charismatic activity was still prominent in the worship and ministry of the church in the second century, but prophetic excess and abuse led to the need for control and a process of gradual institutionalization, with spiritual gifts becoming localized eventually in the offce of the bishop. Clement of Rome and Ignatius of Antioch claimed to be inspired by the Spirit to write to the churches and recognized the operation of spiritual gifts among ordinary Christians. However, both were bishops themselves, and consequently emphasized the importance of obedience to the bishop.

The second century saw the emergence of a tendency to link the activity of the Spirit to ritual performance. Thus water baptism came to be regarded as the seal of the Spirit, and confirmation, administered by the laying on of hands, a further endowment of grace for service. Penance later came to be regarded as a second baptism through which the erring believer's sins are forgiven and the Spirit's seal bestowed afresh. The church fathers in general, however, did their best to distinguish the Spirit's work from the ritual.

Justin Martyr believed all Christians receive the Holy Spirit through faith and water baptism, and that some Christians have received special gifts of the Spirit, including wisdom, prophecy, healing and exorcism. Irenaeus taught that humankind was redeemed by Christ through the regenerating power of the Holy Spirit. He emphasized the Spirit's cleansing work in the hearts and minds of people as he enables them to experience union and fellowship with God. He also recognized the ongoing operation of charismatic gifts in the life of the church, but strongly emphasized the inseparable link between the Spirit and the church.

Clement of Alexandria treated the Spirit as subordinate to both the Father and the Son, and the Holy Spirit as the source of all true knowledge and spiritual gifts. The Spirit is the light and power of the Word, whose voice is heard in the Old and New Testaments. Origen recognized the value of water baptism, but saw it as meaningful only when related to the renewing work of the Spirit. For Origen, the chief function of the Holy Spirit was to promote holiness among believers. The Spirit indwells believers and draws them close to Christ through the study of the Scriptures and their experience of his presence in prayer, which leads them towards spiritual maturity.

Tertullian was the earliest church father to affirm the Holy Spirit's deity clearly. The Holy Spirit, a distinct third 'person' in the Trinity, was sent as the 'Vicar' of Christ and is the interpreter of Scripture. Tertullian's thought is a good illustration of the ongoing tension we observe between Spirit and church. On one hand, he was a committed churchman who took the Christian initiation ceremonies of water baptism and unction (anointing) seriously. At the same time he was attracted to the free pursuit of an experience of the Spirit he observed among the Montanists. He refused to identify the Spirit's bestowal with any external rite, regarding baptism as a sign and seal of repentance that prepares the heart for the Spirit's reception:

> We are not washed in order that we may cease sinning, but because we have ceased from sinning, and in heart have been washed already. . . . Not indeed in the water do we receive the Holy Spirit, but . . . we are by the water of Baptism cleansed and prepared for the Holy Spirit. (Quoted by Burleigh 1954: 115)

Novatian, a sectarian leader and the first Latin writer of the Roman Church, taught that the church is perfected and completed by the presence of the Spirit. The church reaches the required standard of holiness as a result of the operation of the Spirit through his gifts. Hippolytus threw much light on the exercise of spiritual gifts within the established structure of the church. He saw the Spirit as working through church leaders, gifted laity and in the assemblies of believers. He represented the last generation in the West who believed that the Spirit works directly in and through the whole church. By the time of Cyprian, in the second half of the third century, the prophetic element was completely institutionalized. He was the first to connect the seal of the Spirit with the laying on of hands and believed that spiritual gifts are vested in the bishop, who alone has authority to exercise them through the administration of the sacraments.

By the third century much of the apostolic awareness of the Spirit's immediate presence and activity was lost in the reaction to prophetic excess and abuse. Subsequent centuries witnessed the growing institutionalization of the Spirit's work in the church. At the same time, however, there was ongoing acknowledgment of the Spirit's work distinct from yet complementary to church ritual and authority. Thus, in the middle of the fourth century, Cyril of Jerusalem, insists that baptism is efficacious only when accompanied by repentance, faith and piety:

> When you come to the font, do not have regard to the minister of Baptism, be he bishop, priest, or deacon; the grace you will receive is not of men, but of God through the hands of men. But remember the Holy Spirit of whom we have spoken; He is ready to seal your

soul . . . If you play the hypocrite, you may be baptized by men, but
you will not be baptized by the Spirit. But if you come in faith, while
men will administer the visible rite, the Holy Spirit will give you
that which is invisible . . . you will receive power such as you never
had before, you will receive armour at the sight of which evil spirits
tremble. If you believe, you will not only receive remission of sins,
but you will henceforth do things that are beyond human strength.
(Quoted in Swete 1912: 206–207)

Basil of Caesarea, likewise, emphasized the close relation between
baptism and personal faith. Although a thorough sacramentalist, Augustine,
too, regarded the outward rite of baptism as possessing no efficacy without
personal conversion and commitment. The church fathers thus generally
agreed that while the outward seal of authentic Christian faith was baptism,
the inward seal was the active presence of the Holy Spirit.

The original baptismal rite included the laying on of hands, but with
the passage of time water baptism began to be distinguished from a second
rite called 'confirmation'. By the end of the fourth century baptism was
regarded as the means by which sins were cleansed, and confirmation the
occasion for the Spirit's reception in fullness. In the West, baptism came to be
considered as the sacrament of the new birth, and confirmation, a sacrament
of the Holy Spirit's empowerment for spiritual growth and maturity. In both
East and West, Christian initiation was incomplete apart from confirmation.
While the indwelling of the Spirit was thought to begin at baptism, it was in
confirmation that the fullness of the Spirit was bestowed.

This two-stage blessing of the Spirit found endorsement within the
emerging monastic spirituality. Remission of sins was received through
baptism, but the fullness of the Spirit was received only at the time of
dedication to the monastic way of life. The empowering of the Spirit was thus
associated with the monastic vocation, providing for some a vital awareness
of the Holy Spirit. Bernard of Clairvaux and Thomas Aquinas both described
the monastic life as 'a second baptism', restoring the person to a state of
sinless innocence.

An openness to the Spirit's free movement continued within the mystical
tradition, but many theologians and clergymen found greater spiritual security
in the form and order of the church. Some, like Chrysostom and Theodore of
Mopsuestia, maintained that a holy life rather than charismatic gifts was true
evidence of the Spirit's presence. The prophetic tradition was thereafter kept

alive only within some Christian monastic orders and sectarian movements outside Christian orthodoxy.

Sectarian Spirit movements

Even as mainstream Christianity became increasingly sacramental, Spirit movements emerged inside and outside the church that emphasized a direct experience of the Holy Spirit. These movements of religious enthusiasm promised an immediate experience of God that transcended the realm of the material world. In the extreme spirituality of some of these movements, the inner light of individual spiritual experience superseded the authority of Scripture.

Of these movements the most serious threat to the early church was that posed by Gnosticism. Although it flourished from the first to the third centuries ad, elements of Gnostic influence can be traced well into the Middle Ages. The different Gnostic movements shared in common a system of radical dualism: denigration of the material world and corresponding exaltation of the spiritual world. Every human spirit was unalterably divine, imprisoned within an evil body.

Christian Gnostics believed that salvation was through a gift of higher knowledge (*gnōsis*) through the Holy Spirit. Those with this knowledge were given gifts of the Spirit. But the Holy Spirit was viewed, like the Son, as an emanation, subordinate to the Father, and sometimes characterized as the divine mother, the virgin to whom Christ was born. Christian Gnostic sacraments included the unction and sealing of the Holy Spirit, valued above baptism. One of the most influential expressions of Gnosticism was Manichaeism. Its founder, Mani, claimed to be the Holy Spirit based on one of his many revelations. Manichaeism had no sacramental rites: salvation was based on higher knowledge and virtue.

We see a revival of Gnostic teaching between the thirteenth and fifteenth centuries in a movement called the Bogomils, who taught a baptism with the Holy Spirit through the laying on of hands, but without water. They were the precursors of the Cathari or Albigenses, a movement that emerged in the Middle Ages also marked by Gnostic elements. Their rite of 'consolation', administered subsequent to baptism, was conferred by the laying on of hands, and like baptism was regarded as conveying the forgiveness of sins.

A strong revival of ecstatic prophecy came with the rise of Montanism in Asia Minor in the middle of the second century. The Montanists regarded their founder, Montanus, as a mouthpiece of the Holy Spirit and their movement as heralding a new age of the Spirit. They viewed Christian baptism as fulfilled in a baptism of the Spirit, and eagerly reclaimed the gifts of the Spirit, especially prophecy and speaking in tongues. They saw their prophetic utterances as supplanting the Old Testament and New Testament, and maintained that the authority of their prophets replaced the priestly authority of the established church. The rigorous asceticism that marked Montanism was also reflected in other aberrant Spirit movements.

Although Montanism was condemned as a heresy, some scholars regard the movement as a genuine attempt to recapture the vitality of the New Testament church. It has been viewed favourably especially by some Methodists and modern-day Pentecostals. Although the rise of Montanism was a reaction to the growing spiritual and moral laxity in the mainline church, it produced a backlash that effectually stifled the freedom of the Spirit, strengthened the church's authority and reinforced its traditional hierarchy.

Closer to Christian orthodoxy was twelfth-century Joachimism, a restoration movement, founded by Joachim of Fiore, which sought to inaugurate a church of the Spirit similar to the firstcentury church. Joachim taught a three-age conception of history based on the Trinity. The third of these stages, identified with the Holy Spirit and marked by the ascendancy of monastic orders, was imminent: the church would be cleansed of all corruption, ushering in a thousand-year utopia. In contrast to the graded hierarchy of the established church, Joachimism was radically egalitarian. The age of the Spirit the movement heralded was to be an age of peace governed by the Sermon on the Mount. The sacraments would no longer be needed because the Holy Spirit would rule directly over his people. Joachim's vision of historical evolution, where he anticipated a golden era of human freedom and happiness, impacted not just subsequent revival movements, but was extremely influential in helping undergird social struggles for centuries to come, and in shaping the thought of influential secular thinkers like Karl Marx.

Likewise, the fourteenth-century Friends of God was a loose association of people whose beliefs were closer to classical Christian mysticism than Gnosticism. They believed that the direct experience of the Spirit took precedence over ecclesiastical tradition. Charismatic gifts such as ecstasy, prophecy and visions were thus part of their experience of the Spirit. Although free movement of the Spirit was valued over rites and rituals, they sought to exercise a positive influence within the wider church without causing division.

The Catholic Apostolic Church was an early nineteenth century British restorationist movement. Also known as 'Irvingites' after Edward Irving, their most celebrated leader, they protested unsuccessfully against what they regarded as empty traditionalism and lifeless form in the church. However, although they stressed the freedom of the Spirit and experienced spiritual gifts such as tongues, interpretation and prophecy in their services, they also had a place for ritual and the sacraments and used art and symbolism to create the right atmosphere for worship. The sect's genuine attempt to recover the spiritual liberty and power of the New Testament church led them into spiritual excesses and some doctrinal aberrations; as, for instance, the conviction that Christ would return during their lifetime and the belief in a secret rapture of the saints. This movement is widely regarded as a forerunner of twentieth-century Pentecostalism.

The sectarian movements, for the most part, represent unbridled expressions of the prophetic spirit, freedom without form taken to the extreme. Emphasis on a direct experience of the Spirit that does not take scriptural authority seriously, and ignores the biblical obligation to be rightly related and accountable to the church, can lead to fanatical and cultic excesses. This is true even in the twentieth and twenty-first centuries, during which cults have frequently emerged in the wake of revival movements. These have given rise to such bizarre teachings as denying medical attention to the sick in the name of divine healing, and requiring faith to be demonstrated through consumption of poison and handling of poisonous snakes (based on Mark 16:15–18).

Christian mysticism

The impulse for a direct experience of the Spirit expressed itself within both Eastern and Western streams of the church in the form of Christian mysticism. Christian mystics viewed the goal of life not as a higher kind of knowledge (*gnōsis*) but as love, reflected in humble service. Although encouraging deeper commitment to the church rather than separation, Christian mystical spirituality has coexisted in tension with the institutional church, with its emphasis on the hierarchy and sacraments. The church hierarchy thus tended to view the mystics' appeal to direct experience of the Spirit as a threat to their authority. Although Christian mystics affirmed the importance of the sacraments for faith and the spiritual life, they implicitly minimized the need for the church's mediation by their emphasis on the possibility of a direct experience of God beyond outward signs and rituals. However, while insisting that faith involves experience, in general most recognized that faith could at times thrive even in the absence of felt experience.

We thus observe a similar response in the mystics' attitude to the gifts of the Spirit. Spiritual gifts were an integral aspect of the experience of some. Bernard of Clairvaux (12th c.) believed there was an experience of the Holy Spirit beyond conversion and also exercised gifts of healing and miracles. Martin of Tours (4th c.) was a noted healer and exorcist. The Benedictine abbess Hildegard of Bingen (12th c.) was endowed with gifts of healing and counsel. She strongly emphasized the role of the supernatural workings of the Spirit in confirming the truth of the gospel. Francis of Assisi (13th c.) received heavenly visions and dreams. Anthony of Padua (13th c.) was a gifted preacher and worker of miracles. Catherine of Siena (14th c.) displayed gifts of healing, discernment and prophecy. The ministry of Vincent Ferrer (15th c.) included healing, miracles and prophecy. Teresa of Avila (16th c.) was gifted with visions and supernatural wisdom. Her ecstatic experiences sometimes caused her to experience spiritual trances and be lifted up from the floor (Bloesch 2000: 94–95).

On the other hand, most were cautious, even deeply suspicious, towards spiritual gifts. Although they insisted that faith involved experience, they did not make faith contingent on experience. Meister Eckhart and John of the Cross (16th c.) recognized the validity and proper place of gifts, but cautioned against being overly enamoured by them. The gifts must not distract from the centrality of Scripture and are no substitute for faith or loving service of humankind. Brother Lawrence and François Fénelon (17th c.) are also wary of linking faith too closely to the gifts and favours of God, and warn against the pitfall of self-centred exercise of the supernatural gifts:

> These supernatural gifts nourish in secret the life of the old nature. It is an ambition of the most refined character, since it is wholly spiritual. But it is merely ambition, a desire to feel, to enjoy, to possess God and his gifts, to behold his light, to discern spirits, to prophesy – in short, to be an extraordinarily gifted person. For the enjoyment of revelations and delights leads the soul little by little toward a secret coveting of all these things. (Fénelon 1997: 90)

Christian mysticism thus succeeded in keeping alive the impulse within the church for a vibrant experience of the Spirit over and above what the church mediated through its sacramental ritual and hierarchy. It symbolized a genuine attempt to preserve the church's need for vitality and the freedom of the Spirit along with its need for order, structure, authority and accountability.

The Reformation period

The Protestant Reformation represented a movement of the Spirit against the ritualism and formalism of the church, eventually resulting in a movement that separated from the Roman Catholic Church. In what was essentially a revolt against the authority of the established church hierarchy, the Reformers sought to establish their alternative ground of authority in the Bible, expressed in the famous dictum sola scriptura. In so doing they initiated a recovery of a theology of Word and Spirit, which, while freeing the Spirit from being institutionalized by the church, insisted on a robust Christological and soteriological framework for treating the Spirit's identity and activity.

Martin Luther, the best-known Protestant Reformer, viewed the work of the Spirit as closely linked to the Word and sacraments. Thus baptism with water and the Word is a means of grace by which the Spirit cleanses our hearts. At the same time he insists that baptism (which during the period of the Reformers referred almost exclusively to infant baptism) has no salvific value unless it is followed by repentance and faith: it marks the beginning of a salvific process that includes repentance, faith and sanctification. Thus the outward sign of baptism makes no impact in and of itself; it is the spiritual baptism that regenerates us:

> The sacrament, or sign, of baptism is quickly over . . . But the thing it signifies, viz. the spiritual baptism, the drowning of sin, lasts so long as we live, and is completed only in death. Then it is that man is completely sunk in baptism, and that thing comes to pass which baptism signifies. Therefore this life is nothing else than a spiritual baptism which does not cease till death. (Pelikan 1957: 22:287)

Conversion is accompanied by a witness of the Holy Spirit in the experience of the believer. Luther strongly opposed the tendency he observed among the radical Reformers of pursuing inward subjective experiences apart from the Word and the sacraments, and in general did not regard spiritual gifts as having much value (Burgess and van der Maas 2002: 764).

John Calvin, who led the Reformation movement in Geneva, Switzerland, also regarded the bestowal of the Spirit as inseparable from the sacrament of baptism, but stressed even more strongly the necessity of repentance and faith for baptism to be of any value. For Calvin, the primary work of the Holy Spirit is to lead fallen humans to Christ and engraft them into the church. Through the preaching of the Word and the illumination of the Spirit a sinner is effectually called, and then converted through the regenerating work of the Holy Spirit. While Calvin accepts the ongoing need and validity of spiritual gifts in general, the Christian virtues (the fruit of the Spirit, rather than ecstatic gifts) are of greater value as evidence of the authentic Christian life.

Ulrich Zwingli, another leading Reformer who favoured more radical changes in the church, does not restrict the work of the Spirit to the Scriptures and the sacraments. Rather, the Spirit works freely among humans in accordance with God's choice and purpose. He distinguishes clearly between the baptism of the Spirit and water baptism. Spirit baptism is a salvific experience of inner illumination and calling that unites us with God, while the sacraments are outward testimonies to grace rather than actual means of grace. Zwingli was opposed to church hierarchical structures, which he saw as hindering the free flow of the Spirit's grace among the people of God, insisting instead that they be replaced by the authority of the preacher-prophet and magistrate.

The work of the 'magisterial' (or teaching) Reformers like Luther, Calvin and Zwingli, who led the mainstream Reformation, provided the atmosphere for the emergence of radical Reformers. The radical Reformers included the Spiritualists and Anabaptists, whose greater emphasis on the prophetic freedom of the Spirit caused the magisterial Reformers to describe them as religious enthusiasts. The Spiritualists under Thomas Müntzer heralded the dawning of a new age of the Spirit. Müntzer insisted on the necessity of an inner baptism of the Holy Spirit, while rejecting the practice of infant baptism as a meaningless external rite. For Müntzer, the inner word directly illuminated by the Holy Spirit, rather than the letter of Scripture, was the final authority for faith. Scripture was to be interpreted according to the Spirit's guidance rather than pure mental reasoning.

Müntzer was convinced that the powerful vitality that marked the Christian experience of the Holy Spirit in New Testament times should continue to characterize the life of the church in subsequent eras. He believed that God used spiritual gifts to communicate signs of his active presence among his people. Spiritualists thus rejected sacramentalism, believing that baptism should follow rather than precede conversion, and regarding the Lord's Supper as only a memorial of Christ's death. Their greatest weakness was that they tended to dilute the authority of Scripture by the high value they ascribed to their experience of the Spirit.

Like the Spiritualists, the Anabaptists believed in an imminent age of the Spirit and also denied that baptism was a means of grace. Menno Simons, their most influential leader, regarded Christ alone as the pre-eminent sign of grace, and baptism as more a pledge of obedience than a rite of conversion. Water baptism must be administered only to those who have turned to Christ already and been baptized with the Holy Spirit. This marks the beginning of a life guided and empowered by the Holy Spirit, who then reproduces the nature of Christ in the life of the believer. Simons emphasized the Spirit's anointing, through which Christians are bestowed with spiritual gifts. He also taught that the Spirit enables God's will to be expressed through the consensus of the believing community, an important feature of Anabaptist theology and practice in subsequent years.

In addition to the baptism of the Spirit and by water, the Anabaptists also believed in a baptism of fire and blood. Strong emphasis began to be placed on the baptism of blood, generally referring to martyrdom and outward suffering in the world. This was also sometimes applied corporately to the believing community as a whole rather than the individual, the basis of an important emphasis on the suffering of the righteous remnant. This conviction has helped guide subsequent movements for freedom of choice in matters of faith and conscience, and peaceful resistance to repressive and tyrannical authoritarianism either within the church or in civil society.

In contrast to the general scepticism the magisterial Reformers held towards the occurrence of supernatural gifts beyond the apostolic period, the various Anabaptist sects were more open to them. They witnessed many of the occurrences observed in the Pentecostal movement today, including healings, prophecy, tongues and dancing in the Spirit. However, despite some of these similarities with contemporary Pentecostalism, there are marked differences. Most significantly, for Anabaptists, the baptism of the Spirit is primarily associated with salvation and involves suffering; for Pentecostals, Spirit baptism is an endowment of power for ministry, a joyful experience rather than endurance under trial.

The work of the Reformers did provide a timely corrective to the growing formalism and ceremonialism of the Roman Catholic Church. For some, however, their appropriation of the Spirit's work did not go far enough in addressing the needs of those who longed for a palpable heart experience with the Spirit. This was probably what contributed in part to the emergence of several movements of revival and renewal within the church in subsequent centuries.

Winds of spiritual renewal

Several movements of spiritual renewal that first arose in the late sixteenth and early seventeenth centuries continued to impact the spiritual life of the church in succeeding centuries well into the modern era; indeed, right up to the present. These movements all have distinctive emphases, but share in common an impulse we observe throughout the history of the church: an assertion of the Spirit's freedom to work over and above (not necessarily against) the existing formal structures and institutions of the church.

Puritanism was a renewal movement within the Anglican Church towards the end of the sixteenth century that emphasized the importance of spiritual experience. The Puritans sought purity in worship and life and regarded the preaching of the Word as the high point in worship. They opposed images and symbols in worship, but had a high view of the sacraments. The Puritans went beyond Reformation teaching in encouraging believers to expect signs or experiential confirmation of the assurance of salvation. While the Reformers believed that faith alone brings assurance of salvation, the Puritans advocated an inward experience of assurance by the Spirit, which some referred to as a 'sealing' of the Spirit.

The Puritans were concerned primarily with the Spirit's role in the new birth, holiness and the development of spiritual disciplines like prayer. In general, they were cautious towards and sceptical of religious enthusiasm. The Puritans supplemented the Reformation conviction regarding salvation by grace through faith alone with a refreshing emphasis on the need for experiencing the Holy Spirit's power and joy in the Christian life. While some Puritans stayed within the Anglican Communion, others, like John Owen, chose to separate and become Congregationalists.

Pietism was to the Lutheran and Reformed Churches in Europe what Puritanism was to British Anglicanism. Its development was at its peak in the seventeenth and eighteenth centuries but continued to impact European evangelicalism in subsequent centuries. While Pietists acknowledged the effcacy of the Spirit's regenerative work in baptism, they strongly emphasized the importance of personal conversion and the need for the lives of Christians to reflect the fruits of obedience. Although some Pietists made allowance for the gifts of the Spirit in the ministry of the church, in general their attitude to the spiritual gifts was one of cautious suspicion. A revival of Pietist spirituality in the nineteenth century was marked by a Spirit-focused optimism that anticipated the imminent realization over all creation of Christ's conquest of the powers of evil.

A Spirit movement that has made a significant impression on modern Christian spirituality is *Quakerism*. Its founder, George Fox, was a separatist who believed that the final criterion for faith was not Scripture or the creeds but the inner light of the indwelling Spirit in human beings. The Quakers were opposed to the sacraments and insisted on total dependence on the Holy Spirit in worship. They waited in silence for the Spirit to move upon people to pray and prophesy, and often trembled in awe when the Spirit moved upon them. The Quakers encouraged the use of spiritual gifts such as healing and prophecy in public worship. However, their failure to affirm the objective authority and priority of Scripture over subjective spiritual experience resulted in the movement's progressive drift away from biblical faith. Christian Spirit movements today that pursue unusual manifestations of the Spirit thus do well to anchor their teaching and practice judiciously in the authority of Scripture.

Spiritual enthusiasm in the Roman Catholic Church found similar expression in movements such as the *Quietists* in the sixteenth and seventeenth centuries. Quietists taught that passive and quiet submission is the way to a state of perfect union and absorption with God, enabling a person to experience unaided fellowship with God and to live above sin. Quietist ideas have had some influence on the Protestant Holiness movement. A significant movement of spiritual renewal in the Catholic Church was Jansenism, which originated in France in the seventeenth and eighteenth centuries. Although the movement tended towards a legalistic moralism, it emphasized a warm personal faith, perhaps best reflected in the teaching of its most famous proponent, Blaise Pascal, that the heart, not reason, experiences God.

Evangelicalism is a term with a broad range of connotations, but I use it here to refer to the spiritual awakening in Britain and the American colonies in the mid-eighteenth century, followed by the wider evangelical revival movement of the nineteenth and twentieth centuries (Bloesch 2000: 125). The Protestant Reformation, Puritanism and Pietism are the principal sources from which the evangelical movement has drawn its inspiration. A key leader in the eighteenth-century evangelical awakening was John Wesley, who not only founded Methodism, but whose influence also extended to the later Holiness and Pentecostal movements. In contrast to Calvinism, Wesley made considerable room for the cooperation of the human will in conversion. He emphasized the experiential dimension of sanctification as a 'second blessing' subsequent and complementary to justification, describing this experience in terms of entire sanctification or Christian perfection. Wesley was favourably disposed towards the Montanists and was not opposed to the exercise of spiritual gifts and emotional expression in worship. But he insisted that the genuineness of all spiritual experiences be tested based on their Christ-centredness and faithfulness to scriptural teaching.

George Whitefield and Jonathan Edwards were representative of the Calvinistic emphasis within the eighteenth-century evangelical awakening. While insisting on the importance of experiential religion, they emphasized the continuing ongoing work of the Spirit rather than a 'second blessing'. While eagerly anticipating a widespread outpouring of the Holy Sprit, Edwards was cautious about the manifestation of supernatural gifts. He viewed these as characteristic of spiritual infancy, while true Christian maturity was demonstrated by the fruits of obedience and Christlike graces.

We see a similar difference in perspective regarding the 'second blessing' among evangelicals in later years. Charles Simeon and Abraham Kuyper were among those who espoused the Calvinist position regarding the Spirit's work, while the Wesleyan emphasis continued to find expression in the ministry of Dwight L. Moody, R. A. Torrey and John Hyde, among others. But common emphases that continue to unite the evangelical movement include the authority of Scripture, the decisiveness of Christ and his substitutionary atonement, salvation by grace through faith and the need for personal conversion, the imminent personal return of Christ and the urgency of the missionary mandate.

The *Holiness movement* has its roots in the emphasis within Methodism on a second sanctifying crisis experience of grace subsequent to conversion. This was sometimes described in later years as the baptism of the Holy Spirit. The Holiness movement, however, has features that clearly distinguish it from the Methodist position in several areas. In contrast to Wesley's positive attitude to the sacraments, the spirituality of the Holiness movement has no place for the sacraments. Proponents of the Holiness movement are much more optimistic about the degree of sinless perfection attainable through the second blessing than Wesley, whose view of sanctification was considerably tempered and more realistic. While Wesley viewed justification and sanctification as free and gracious gifts of God that cannot be earned, the Holiness movement frequently appears to insist on a certain degree of practical holiness as a requirement for salvation.

The Holiness emphasis gave rise to several new church movements, including the Salvation Army, the Christian and Missionary Alliance, the Church of the Nazarene, the Free Methodist Church and the Church of God. Two leaders of the Christian and Missionary Alliance who had a key role in shaping the Holiness movement were its founder, A. B. Simpson, and the well-known Bible teacher A. W. Tozer. Tozer was convinced of the need to be filled with the Spirit, but did not subscribe to the instant crisis experience teaching promoted within popular revivalism. He emphasized instead the importance of a consistent lifelong walk in the Spirit, nurtured by a deep love for and dependence on the study of the Scriptures:

> the Spirit of truth cannot and does not operate apart from the letter of the Holy Scriptures. For this reason a growing acquaintance with the Holy Spirit will always mean an increasing love for the Bible. The Scriptures are in print what Christ is in person. The inspired Word is like a faithful portrait of Christ. . . . From this it follows naturally that a true lover of God will be also a lover of His Word. Anything that comes to us from the God of the Word will deepen our love for the Word of God. (Quoted by Wiersbe 1978: 188–189)

Despite its distinctly Methodist origins, with time, Holiness ideas filtered into Presbyterian and Baptist circles. The Presbyterian evangelist Charles Finney was convinced of the necessity of a second baptism of the Holy Spirit that brings sanctification. The South African Reformed preacher Andrew Murray believed that the baptism of the Holy Spirit does not eradicate sin from within the life of believers, but enables them to resist sin. Oswald Chambers, a Scottish Baptist minister, taught that the baptism of the Spirit both sanctifies the believer and empowers for witness. For others like the Baptist evangelist and Bible teacher J. Sidlow Baxter, entire sanctification, a second blessing after regeneration, involves not the eradication of sin but an infilling of the Spirit.

Pentecostalism is undoubtedly the most significant movement of the Spirit in the twentieth century, and constitutes today the largest Protestant grouping in the world. The growth of Pentecostalism to an estimated 500 million adherents within a century of its birth as a modern movement has provoked considerable scholarly interest. While the most significant growth of Pentecostalism has occurred in Latin America, Africa and Asia,

Pentecostalism can be found today in almost every corner of the globe. Pentecostalism has experienced greatest receptivity among the poor and working classes all over the world. However, the growth of the movement in Western nations is marginal compared to its exponential growth rate in the nonWestern world.

There is an amazing degree of diversity among Pentecostal churches and movements. While a significant stream of Pentecostalism has its roots in American classical Pentecostal and independent charismatic churches, the roots of most other streams are in spontaneous indigenous movements of the Spirit within local contexts, largely independent of Western influences. Pentecostalism thus does not represent uniform doctrine, cultural homogeneity or organizational unity. It rather consists of multifarious streams and a wide variety of expressions across the globe.

Pentecostalism is best defined in terms of its single most distinguishing feature: the central place ascribed to a life-transforming experience of God the Holy Spirit. Thus what unites the different expressions of Pentecostalism globally is its common spirituality, which includes an emphasis on experiential spirituality, the exercise of spiritual gifts, especially glossolalia and divine healing, fervent worship and prayer, a high view of the Bible, vocational empowerment and participation of all believers in ministry, conservative morality and urgency of mission.

Despite a distinctive understanding of the work of the Holy Spirit, the deep roots of Pentecostalism in Scripture and Christian tradition are being increasingly acknowledged. The recognition within the Holiness movement of the baptism of the Holy Spirit as a second crisis experience subsequent to conversion clearly prepared the way for the Pentecostal revival. Pentecostalism was born when this experience was linked to speaking in tongues and with the power to witness rather than sanctification. Most Pentecostal groups today maintain that sanctification is a progressive walk rather than a crisis experience.

The phenomenal growth of the Pentecostal movement globally makes a sober assessment of future challenges and opportunities a critical need. The movement's strengths have been widely acknowledged, and include Christ-centredness, joyful worship, warm and spontaneous fellowship, emphasis on every-member ministry, generous giving and a passionate commitment to mission. The enormous potential of the movement could be maximized if significant weaknesses were addressed effectively (Packer 2005: 151–159). The tendencies towards sectarianism, emotionalism and obsession with supernatural experience are all rooted in an anti-intellectualism that persists in many quarters despite the growing number of scholars within the Pentecostal movement. There is, however, a welcome self-critique emerging, illustrated in the following passionate plea from a young Pentecostal theologian:

> We ought to acknowledge that reason and logic are gifts from God;
> that the mind and intellect are, in large measure, his image in us . . .
> Far too long, Pentecostals and Charismatics have maintained that
> true Bible believing Christians should be suspect of the intellect.
> It is time to turn back the tide, prevail over this self-induced injury
> . . . Our goal, then, is to continue to fan the fires of Pentecost with
> passion while at the same time endeavoring to cultivate the gardens
> of our minds with care and persistence. (Nanez 2005: 26)

A number of helpful insights emerge from this brief survey of the Spirit's activity in the life of the church over the last twenty centuries. It is the Spirit's presence and activity that clearly distinguish the church as the people of God, but what are the marks of the Spirit's presence and how do we discern his activity?

We have seen that the life of the church from New Testament times to the present reflects a certain tension between those who would like to see the Spirit's activity restricted to the church, and others who view church structure, form and ritual as stifling celebration of the Spirit's freedom. On one hand, we have seen that it is impossible to 'domesticate' the blessed Holy Spirit. From time to time he raises movements outside the organized church that issue prophetic calls to the people of God to return to authentic Christianity, which they seem to have abandoned, and to awake from their spiritual stupor. There is in fact very little about the Spirit's activity in the church throughout the ages that may be regarded as radically innovative. Many of the emphases we observe within contemporary revival movements are in keeping with the Spirit experience of the New Testament church, Montanism, the Reformers, the Anabaptists, the Evangelical and Holiness movements and other Spirit movements of the previous centuries. This observation should help us understand and be more accepting of movements we may otherwise regard as eccentric and cultic.

On the other hand, we have also observed that the Spirit's freedom was liable frequently to misuse and perversion through prophetic excesses and abuse of charismatic gifts. The reaction to this gave rise to structures of authority and accountability within the church, which led inevitably to control and institutionalization. But whenever the church has allowed the Spirit's free activity, he continues to persevere with the church, even working through its structures and institutions. Thus, although we have observed the emergence of Spirit movements both within and outside the organized church, we must recognize that the Spirit has never given up on the church even in its darkest and most difficult moments.

As God has designed it, the Holy Spirit and the church, the community of the Spirit, should be inseparable. But the church must never take this truth for granted, or complacently assume that the Spirit will continue to remain and work within the church regardless of whether or not the Word is consistently taught and practised. Church history is replete with illustrations of how churches can compromise allegiance to biblical faith, cease to reflect to the world any signs of kingdom life and mission, and eventually fall into a state of decline and apostasy. However, the fact remains that the church cannot be the church apart from the Holy Spirit, and the Spirit always seeks to work within some expression of the covenant people of God, either within or outside the borders of the organized church.

What, then, are we to conclude from our observations concerning this tension between freedom and form in the way in which the Spirit functions? An important lesson to be learned was brought home to me simply and clearly in the following testimony I heard recently from a bishop of the (episcopal) Church of North India. He recounted his experience when visiting one of the churches in his diocese. Early in the service he began to observe that the form and order of worship was somewhat unconventional. During a time of exuberant singing led by the priest and a worship team, some of the worshippers began to pull out flags and wave them as they sang. He was at first rather disturbed by the departure from the regular order of service and the unusually enthusiastic expressions of worship. He was especially anxious that the enthusiasm of the singers seemed to be prolonging the service, and that important elements of the liturgy such as confession of sin and intercessory prayer leading up to the communion service were likely to be neglected. He was also a little troubled about how his response would be perceived if as visiting bishop he were to ignore this deviation from the standard order of worship.

The bishop then called the priest aside and expressed his discomfort at the direction of the service. The priest was quick to reassure him that some of the liturgical elements had been consciously incorporated in the choice of congregational hymns and songs. As the service continued the bishop found himself appreciating the sincere fervour and wholehearted participation of the congregation in the service. By his own admission he began to feel ashamed about his earlier attitude and was deeply convicted about having nearly stifled a genuine expression of Christian devotion. Needless to say, he participated enthusiastically in the rest of the service, thus warmly endorsing what he subsequently acknowledged as a genuine work of the Spirit.

The bishop's pastoral visit concluded with the parish and priest being greatly encouraged and strengthened. But an alternative scenario was also possible. What would have been the outcome of a more rigid approach to the situation? Inevitably, some amount of misunderstanding, hurt and alienation of the priest and congregation. It may have resulted in strife and division, and possibly grieved the Holy Spirit. Instead, the bishop left having earned the love and respect of one of his parishes as a man of God who not only honoured the sentiments of his people but also revered the workings of the Holy Spirit. But he did this without compromising his concern for order and abdicating his duty as bishop.

It was impossible to listen to the testimony of the good bishop without feeling a sense of deep admiration and respect for his humility and wise leadership. But his response illustrates profoundly and beautifully how freedom and form do not necessarily have to be at cross purposes; rather, they can and must converge so that the Spirit's life-giving power may build up the church and further God's purpose. The Holy Spirit is a Spirit of freedom and order, and hence the two must be held closely together. An overemphasis on one to the exclusion of the other can lead to a flawed understanding and deficient experience of the Spirit.

In introducing the concluding synthesis of his rigorous and comprehensive treatment of Pauline pneumatology, Gordon Fee makes this very pertinent observation:

> Historically, Spirit movements have a poor track record within the boundaries of more traditional ecclesiastical structures. From my perspective the fault lies on both sides: reformers tend to burn structures and try to start over (and when they do they only create a new set of structures for the next Spirit movement to burn down); those with vested interests in the structures consequently tend to push Spirit movements to the fringe – or outside altogether. Thus there is a hardening of 'orthodoxy', on the one hand, that tends to keep the Spirit safely domesticated within creeds and office; on

the other hand, when Spirit movements are forced (or choose) to exist outside the proven tradition(s) of the historic church, there is a frequent tendency to throw theological caution to the wind. The result all too often is a great deal of finger pointing and name-calling, without an adequate attempt to embrace both the movement of the Spirit and existing tradition(s) simultaneously. (Fee 1994: 799–800)

An understanding of the church's experience of the Holy Spirit over the last two thousand years helps avoid such needless polarization, and is thus a critical resource for our understanding of how the Spirit works today. We have seen that a wide range of viewpoints on the nature and form of Christian spirituality have emerged in the course of twenty centuries of the church's experience of the Spirit. The Holy Spirit, it seems, works through the sacraments and apart from the sacraments. While some Christians are open to the exercise of the gifts of the Spirit, others favour the Spirit's graces and moral virtues, and the Holy Spirit endows both with his blessings. The Spirit sends the refreshing rain of revival to both Reformed and Wesleyan revival movements alike, despite the differences in their understanding of how the Spirit works. This survey of the church's experience of the Spirit thus provides us with a glimpse into the tapestry of interpretations that comprise the church's rich Spirit tradition. It is against this backdrop that we begin to look in the following chapter at the biblical teaching concerning the Holy Spirit's person and work.

3

I Will Pour Out My Spirit

The Spirit as the Fulfilment of Promise

It is the night of Jesus' betrayal. He is giving his farewell instructions to his disciples in the light of his imminent departure, and makes this promise: 'And I will ask the Father, and he will give you another Counsellor . . . I will not leave you as orphans; I will come to you' (John 14:16, 18). He refers to this promise several times in this farewell discourse (John 14:26; 15:26; 16:7–8, 13). Again, after the resurrection, the last words of Jesus, according to Luke's account, are a reiteration of the promise 'I am going to send you what my Father has promised . . .' (Luke 24:49; cf. Acts 1:4–5, 8). In the Acts description, Jesus uses the term 'baptize' in speaking of the coming of the Holy Spirit, recalling in that expression John the Baptist's earlier prediction, contrasting John's own baptism with water for repentance with the coming Messiah's baptism with the Holy Spirit and fire (Luke 3:16; cf. John 1:32–33). John the Baptist was not, however, the originator of this promise.

We look ahead to Acts 2, which gives us a vivid description of what happened in the upper room on the day of Pentecost. The church was born as a result of a dramatic outpouring of the Holy Spirit on the hundred and twenty disciples who were waiting for the promised Holy Spirit. All Jerusalem was in an uproar, as these unlearned Galilean disciples spoke in various Asian, African and European languages, which the large number of non-resident Jews in Jerusalem to celebrate the feast, were able to recognize. Distraught and confused, they asked the obvious question *What does this mean?*

Peter's response grounds this event in the Old Testament prediction of the Spirit's universal outpouring in Joel 2, and links it to the earthly ministry, death, resurrection and exaltation of Jesus, asserting that as a consequence of

Christ's finished work, 'he has received the promise of the Holy Spirit which he has then poured out upon his disciples' (Acts 2:33). Peter himself clarifies that this promise of the Holy Spirit is meant not just for a special group of people or for his own generation but for 'for all whom the Lord our God will call' (Acts 2:39). But in Galatians 3:13–14, Paul asserts clearly that through Christ's redemptive work, the Gentiles are able to partake of the blessing God promised to Abraham, and that the substance of the promised blessing is the bestowal of the Holy Spirit. So the promise of the Holy Spirit Jesus makes to his disciples prior to his departure from this earth was originally the promise God gave to Israel.

Jesus thus refers to the bestowal of the Holy Spirit as 'the gift my Father promised' (Acts 1:4). What is in focus, then, is the promise of God himself regarding the Holy Spirit made originally to ancient Israel and then consummated at the outpouring of his Spirit on the day of Pentecost. What was the Old Testament experience like? What images, concepts and traditions from the Old Testament experience shaped the early Christian anticipation of the Holy Spirit's outpouring? Essential for a full-orbed biblical understanding of the Holy Spirit is that we first pay attention to the Old Testament description of the Spirit's nature and activity.

The Spirit in the Old Testament

Although the Spirit is never identified explicitly with God in the Old Testament, he is so closely linked with God as to be a part of him. He is God's enabling power, God's breath that gives life to men, controls and guides them to act.

The Hebrew word for 'spirit', *rûah*, has two basic meanings, 'wind' and 'breath', and is used in three different ways to denote (1) *wind:* a stream of air or breath of air; (2) *the soul:* the principle of life or breath, the individual human consciousness; and (3) *the divine Spirit:* the life of God himself, the force by which God acts. Its specific identification as the Spirit *of God* is made based on the qualification or context. The term always connotes a dynamic reality, power in action and denotes God's active, powerful presence. The Spirit manifests personal qualities such as a capacity to guide, to instruct and to be grieved (Ps. 143:10; Neh. 9:20; Isa. 63:10), but the Old Testament writers do not conceive of 'the Spirit of God' in any way that would compromise their strict monotheism, and thus do not describe him as a distinct person in the sense that the New Testament writers and later Christians did.

However, a clear identification of the 'Holy Spirit' with the Old Testament 'Spirit of God' may be observed in several New Testament passages. According to the New Testament writers, it was the Holy Spirit who gave the children of Israel instructions for ceremonial service (Heb. 9:8), and whom they resisted later during their wilderness journey (Acts 7:51). Likewise, the 'Spirit of God' who gave the inspired word to David, Isaiah and Jeremiah is identified as the 'Holy Spirit' in the New Testament (Mark 12:36; Acts 1:16; 28:25; Heb. 3:7–9; 10:15). The same Holy Spirit predicted Christ's sufferings through the Old Testament prophets and inspired them to record such revelation (1 Pet. 1:11; 2 Pet. 1:21). Peter identifies Joel's promise of the outpouring of God's Spirit with the advent of the Holy Spirit on the day of Pentecost (Acts 2:16–18; cf. Joel 2:28–29). Consequently, just as we regard the Old Testament God as triune based on New Testament teaching, we can read Old Testament references to the Spirit of God in the light of the New Testament disclosure of the Spirit's distinct personhood.

The Old Testament teaching regarding the Spirit is focused essentially around four themes: his role in creation, in the equipping of charismatic leadership, in prophetic inspiration and in messianic expectations. We accordingly see the Spirit in the Old Testament as the *creative Spirit*, the *enabling Spirit*, the *prophetic Spirit* and the *messianic Spirit*. All these ideas find clearer and fuller expression in the New Testament as well as in the later life of the church.

The creative Spirit

The role of the Spirit in creation is a largely neglected theme in Christian treatments of the Spirit's work. In fact, he is present and active in creation, in its origin, sustenance and perfection. A number of Scripture passages speak of the Spirit's role in creation. In the account of creation in Genesis, we read, 'Now the earth was formless and empty, darkness was over the surface of the deep, and the Spirit of God was hovering over the waters' (Gen. 1:2).

The term translated 'to hover' (cf. Deut. 32:11) conveys the idea that the Spirit of God was preserving the unformed earth in preparation for the further creative activity of God described in the rest of the chapter. Concluding a hymn that celebrates the wonders of creation, the psalmist says:

> When you send your Spirit, they are created,
> and you renew the face of the earth.
> (Ps. 104:30)

The 'breath of his mouth' in Psalm 33:6 also probably refers to the Spirit's activity in creation. Job 26:13 describes specifically the Spirit's role in beautifying the heavens. According to Genesis 2:7, the Spirit had a specific function in the creation of man: the breath of life or the stream of life the Spirit imparted made man a living soul. This thought is underlined in Job 33:4: 'The Spirit of God has made me . . .' (cf. Job 27:3). The Spirit is thus the source of physical and spiritual life. God the Spirit is continually creating and ceaselessly active in directing the processes of the natural world.

An appreciation of the Spirit's role in creation should heighten our awareness of God and enhance our worship. All of creation reflects the creative presence and power of the Spirit. For too long the Spirit has been restricted to the private devotional life, mystical spirituality and extraordinary supernatural manifestations. The Spirit's role in creation ensures he is everywhere and must not be excluded from any aspect of human experience. Lederle thus laments the fact that

> For too long the Spirit and his work has been conceived of in too limited a sense . . . The Spirit should not be limited to spiritual experiences and charisms . . . The Spirit is at work in the world and should not be degraded to an ornament of piety. (Lederle 1988: 338)

The well-known Indian Christian mystic Sundar Singh used the expression 'Book of Nature' in trying to describe how creation drew him closer to God, in an obvious comparison with the devotional impact of the Bible. He loved the beauty of nature, it enhanced his communion with God and he drew great enjoyment from observing the great truths of God within the 'Book of Nature'. For him the common authorship of the Holy Spirit ensured continuity between the message of the 'Book of Nature' and the Bible:

> The Bible and the Book of Nature are both written in spiritual language by the Holy Spirit. The Holy Spirit being the author of life, all Nature, instinct with life, is the work of the Holy Spirit, and the language in which it is written is spiritual language. . . . [For those who are born again] the language of the Bible and of nature is their mother tongue, which they easily and naturally understand . . . (Quoted by Streeter and Appasamy 1987: 191–194)

The Bible and the 'Book of Nature' both have the same author, the Holy Spirit, and use the same spiritual language of the Spirit, which only the 'born again' understand. If our spiritual antennas are properly tuned, the Spirit will speak through the most surprising circumstances: the awesome thunderclap, the chirp of the sparrow, the web of the spider. The lives of believers can thus be immeasurably enriched when we are open to encounter the Spirit in the life of creation itself, in nature's beauty and vitality, as well as its flaws.

The presence and activity of the Spirit of God in creation has critical ethical implications, and constitutes the basis for responsible social, economic, political and ecological involvement in our world. We live in a world that, on one hand, under the influence of unbridled raw materialism exploits and ravages the world's natural resources. On the other hand, the impact of Western idealism and Eastern mysticism causes others to deify the world. Recognition of the Spirit's role in creation is a helpful corrective to these two extreme postures of destruction or deification in relation to the natural world. The presence and activity of the Spirit causes us to affirm the essential reality and goodness of creation, but also ensures we distinguish between the created world and the creator of the world. This also provides a basis for responsible sociopolitical engagement through participation in poverty alleviation, development activity, nation-building and global environmental concerns.

Awareness of the Spirit's role in creation thus places significant obligations upon the believer for stewardship and witness. Although the work of creation is complete in the sense that God has called it forth and it exists, it remains incomplete and unfinished in that its goal has not been reached. Now we see creation marred by sin and hence imperfect and provisional. We shall see only at the end of the age, when the Spirit renews creation, the natural order as it was meant to be. The Christian is thus called to involvement in the stewardship of the world and its resources.

The creator Spirit helps maintain a vital link between creation and redemption. All of creation falls within the scope of the Spirit's operations. His role in creation is foundational and prior to all his other activities. Redemption is a restoration of creation, not its negation. The Spirit who redeems is the same Spirit who first creates. Recognition of this essential continuity between the Spirit's creative and redemptive functions provides a basis for the believer's meaningful engagement with people of other faiths or no faith. While our allegiance to Christ's lordship clearly distinguishes Christians from non-Christians, our common humanity and the fact that we are all created in the image of God provides us substantial common ground. This is a theme explored in some detail by Ida Glaser in another excellent volume in this series (Glaser 2005: 54–77). Our attempts to witness to people of other faiths will be much more effective when we recognize and affirm this common ground prior to communicating our faith in Christ.

The Spirit is thus present and active everywhere in creation and we dare not distance ourselves from any realm of his activity. The challenge, of course, is to be able to recognize where he is at work.

The enabling Spirit

A second theme that emerges in the early descriptions of the Spirit's activity in the Old Testament is that of charismatic enablement. The Spirit thus comes upon select individuals to equip them for specific tasks, especially for various leadership roles, such as leading the people of God in battle, and judging and ruling them during times of peace.

Joseph

Joseph is recognized as endowed with the Spirit of God (Gen. 41:38) due to his gift of interpreting dreams. In this context, his endowment is manifested in a charismatic gift, placed in the service of the king and the good of the people. His gift becomes the basis for his being judged a 'discerning and wise man' (Gen. 41:33, 39), whom Pharaoh then chooses to appoint as chief administrator over all of Egypt (Gen. 41:40–44). Can we ask God to endow individuals with his Spirit so they can rule wisely and efficiently? Joseph's experience seems to provide a basis for us to do so. The Spirit anoints political rulers, enabling them to administer honestly and responsibly.

Bezalel and Oholiab

The chief contractor for the construction of the tabernacle was Bezalel, who was given a special enablement of the Spirit for his task. God says to Moses:

> And I have filled him with the Spirit of God, with skill, ability and
> knowledge in all kinds of crafts – to make artistic designs for work
> in gold, silver and bronze, to cut and set stones, to work in wood,
> and to engage in all kinds of craftsmanship. (Exod. 31:3–5)

Both Bezalel and his assistant, Oholiab (Exod. 31:6), were supernaturally endowed with all the skills needed to work on the tabernacle and to teach others to do what was needed as well (Exod. 35:30–36:1).

Some Christians often make the mistake of restricting the Spirit's influence to the so-called sacred sphere – private devotional life and church life. We see, however, that Bezalel and Oholiab's gifts enhanced their creative skills, extending to craftsmanship in wood, stone and metal work. In explaining the significance of this endowment of the Spirit, especially as it applies to the 'secular' sphere, the Old Testament scholar Chris Wright concludes:

> The creation narrative . . . portrays God himself as the universal Master Craftsman, who rejoices in the goodness and beauty of all he has so wonderfully designed and executed. This text encourages us to believe that the same Spirit of God who was at work in creation is also at work in that same wider sense: in all those who, as human beings made in God's image, enrich our world with all kinds of creativity in art, music, colourful design, beautiful craftsmanship and . . . skilful speech and writing. When we honour and admire such art, we give glory to the Spirit who empowers it. (Wright 2006: 39)

The Spirit's scope of activity is thus not restricted to bestowing gifts within the church. He is the creator Spirit who can breathe life into the creative expression of the author, artist, musician, poet, actor, dancer, journalist, advertising executive or any other vocation, especially when pursued in dependence on the Spirit's creative enablement.

Moses and the seventy elders

The children of Israel were moving from Sinai to Kadesh-barnea when God instructed Moses to select seventy elders to help him administer the people. Moses' own endowment with the Spirit is assumed, for its occasion and manner are not described in Scripture. However, here God instructs Moses to bring the seventy elders out to the Tent of Meeting, promising to equip them with the same divine enablement he had given to Moses: 'I will take of the Spirit that is on you and put the Spirit on them. They will help you carry the burden of the people so that you will not have to carry it alone' (Num. 11:17). The fulfilment of this promise is described later in the chapter: 'Then the Lord . . . took of the Spirit that was on him [Moses] and put the Spirit on the seventy elders. When the Spirit rested on them, they prophesied . . .' (Num. 11:25).

Joshua

Joshua was probably included among the elders on this occasion, and then went on to become Moses' successor. He was described by God at the time of his appointment as 'a man in whom is the Spirit' (Num. 27:18), and at the time of his succession following Moses' death, as a person 'filled with the Spirit of wisdom' (Deut. 34:9).

Two of the elders who had not gone out to the Tent of Meeting with the others also experienced the Spirit's endowment and began to prophesy in the camp (Num. 11:26). While Joshua tries to get Moses to suppress this manifestation, Moses perhaps expresses more precisely the divine intention when he says, 'I wish that all the Lord's people were prophets and that the Lord would put his Spirit on them!' (Num. 11:28–29). Both the incident itself as well as Moses' open-handed response to Joshua's attempt to curb this 'out of order' manifestation, suggest that God's benevolence sometimes allows his Spirit to work outside channels or structures he himself has created. His statement also anticipates the prophetic vision announced several centuries later of a universal outpouring of the Holy Spirit (Joel 2:28–29).

Although not much is said here regarding the precise nature or content of the prophetic gift manifested, it was probably a form of ecstatic prophecy prevalent in early Israelite history. We see other illustrations of such ecstatic prophecy in the book of Numbers in the oracles of *Balaam*. In the first two oracles, the Lord is said to have put a 'word' or message in Balaam's mouth (Num. 23:5, 16), but the third oracle is described as the result of the Spirit of God acting upon him (Num. 24:2). Some of the features of ecstatic prophecy are alluded to in the oracle itself: 'the oracle of one whose eye sees clearly, the oracle of one who hears the words of God, who sees a vision from the Almighty, who falls prostrate, and whose eyes are opened' (Num. 24:3–4).

Thus what is in view here is a clear illustration of the convergence of the 'Word of God' and 'Spirit of God' in prophetic activity. God's 'Spirit' rushes upon the prophetic spokesman, placing God's 'Word' in his mouth and enabling him to speak God's message. While descriptions of the first two oracles highlight the means by which God's message is conveyed, the account of the third oracle emphasizes the enabling role of the Spirit. A feature of special interest is that the person used as an instrument of the Spirit to speak God's message, unlike all those we have considered thus far, was not an Israelite. Can an unbeliever ever be used as a vehicle of God's Spirit and a channel of God's message? We shall need to return to this question at a later point in our study.

Judges

During the 150 years from the occupation of Canaan by Joshua until the institution of the monarchy, Israel was a loose federation of tribes. This period saw the emergence of charismatic leaders upon whom the 'Spirit of the Lord' came especially in times of crisis, enabling them to lead and provide deliverance for the people of Israel. Four courageous leaders have their heroic exploits attributed to empowerment by 'the Spirit of the Lord'.

Othniel (Judg. 3:7–11) was the first judge of Israel after the death of Joshua. The Spirit of the Lord (Judg. 3:10) gave Othniel military skill to lead the children of Israel to victory against Mesopotamian aggression, and enabled him to lead Israel for the next forty years. Although Deborah's leadership is not explicitly attributed to the Spirit of God, such an association is clearly implied in her characterization as a prophetess (Judg. 4:4). She judged Israel and, with Barak, also led Israel to victory over the Canaanites who had oppressed Israel for twenty years.

Gideon (Judg. 6:1–8:35) delivered the children of Israel from seven years of oppression by the Midianites. The Spirit of the Lord (Judg. 6:34) empowered him to lead a small band of warriors to overthrow a vast Midianite army through a unique God-given strategy, and also to judge Israel for forty years.

Jephthah (Judg. 10:6–12:7) was enabled by the Spirit of the Lord (Judg. 11:29) to gather a fighting force of Israelites to defeat their Ammonite oppressors, after which he judged Israel for six years.

Samson (Judg. 13:1–16:31), who judged Israel for twenty years is, perhaps, the most notorious judge of Israel. Set apart by a Nazirite vow even before his birth, Samson's exceptional physical strength was associated with his hair, a visible sign of his vow. But the biblical account records that 'the Spirit of the Lord began to stir him' sometime early in his life (Judg. 13:25), and then notes three occasions when 'the Spirit of the Lord came upon him in power' (Judg. 14:6, 19; 15:14). On each of these occasions the Spirit's action was accompanied by extraordinary bursts of power by which he tore a lion apart with his bare hands, broke into a Philistine stronghold and killed thirty men, and went on a rampage, striking down a thousand Philistines with the jawbone of a donkey.

The activity of the Spirit of the Lord in the period of the judges is clearly related to the repentance and supplication of the people of Israel. In response to their cries for deliverance God raised up charismatic leaders to set the people free from their oppressors (Judg. 3:9; 4:3; 6:7; 10:10). However, the Spirit's empowerment of individuals during this period was focused almost exclusively on a specific purpose: bestowing physical strength and courage in battle, to enable military victories and deliverance from political oppression. There is little evidence of moral change or ethical impact in the lives of the judges of Israel resulting from the Spirit's bestowal upon them.

Saul

The story of Saul's anointing by Samuel (1 Sam. 9:26–10:13) links the prophetic office from its inception with the institution of the monarchy. The authority of the king in Israel is shown to derive from the 'Spirit of the Lord' rather than temporal power or pure dynastic succession. The Spirit's bestowal is associated closely with the ritual of anointing, although there is a time lapse between the ritual and the experience. A definite change of heart accompanies the ritual, but the Spirit comes upon him in power when Saul encounters a band of prophets, following which he is caught up in a state of religious fervour and begins to prophesy with them.

The tambourines, flutes and harps mentioned in this account suggest the association of music with prophetic ecstasy (1 Sam. 10:5). In later years, we see David's music on the harp providing Saul relief from a tormenting evil spirit (1 Sam. 16:14–23), and Elisha asking for a harpist in preparation for his exercise of the prophetic gift (2 Kgs 3:15). Is there a basis here for associating music with receptivity to the work of the Holy Spirit? Paul exhorts the Ephesian believers to be filled with the Spirit, and the outcome will be that they 'Speak to one another with psalms, hymns and spiritual songs. Sing and make music in your heart to the Lord, always giving thanks to God the Father for everything . . .' (Eph. 5:19–20). Commenting on this text, John Stott says, 'Without doubt Spirit-filled Christians have a song of joy in their hearts, and Spirit-filled public worship is a joyful celebration of God's mighty acts . . .' (Stott 1979: 206). The fact is that most revivals in church history have been accompanied by renewed devotion and joy in worship, especially among young people, a feature that may be observed among growing churches even today.

The Spirit of the Lord did attest Saul's leadership on occasion, enabling him to rule decisively and zealously (1 Sam. 11:6), but departed from him after God rejected him as Israel's king due to his persistent disobedience (1 Sam. 16:14). 1 Samuel records an instance when the Spirit returns to Saul briefly and temporarily (19:18–24). This appears to have been a sovereign act of God, to counter Saul's jealous and murderous pursuit of David, and display his protection and approval of David. Saul was clearly not in right relationship with God on this occasion, and hence this action of the Spirit was in no way indicative of God's favour.

David

In the account of David's ordination as king, the bestowal of the Spirit is more closely associated with the anointing ritual: the action of the Spirit upon David comes directly as a result of his anointing by the prophet Samuel (1 Sam. 16:13). His empowerment by the Spirit enabled David to rule Israel for forty years. David sinned against God by committing adultery with Bathsheba and arranging to have her husband, Uriah, killed in battle. In his prayer of confession and repentance, he pleads with God:

> Do not cast me from your presence
> or take your Holy Spirit from me.
> (Ps. 51:11)

David knew how God's Spirit had left Saul after he sinned and did not want the same thing to happen to him.

This is one of only three occasions when the title 'Holy Spirit' is used in the Old Testament (cf. Isa. 63:10, 11). The Spirit is holy because he is God, but the Old Testament does not emphasize holiness in the sense of inward moral purity or ethical perfection. The Old Testament emphasis is normally on legal or ceremonial holiness in the sense of that which is separated or set apart for God and his service.

The Spirit continued to work through David, as indicated by the Spirit showing him the pattern for the temple, which he then shared with Solomon (1 Chr. 28:12), and his realization that he was a Spirit-inspired mouthpiece for God:

> The Spirit of the Lord spoke through me;
> his word was on my tongue.
> (2 Sam. 23:2; cf. Acts 1:16)

The period of the monarchy represents the early stages of the institutionalization of the Spirit's presence. The Spirit was believed to remain with God's anointed representative until his kingship ceased, signifying an ongoing link between the Spirit and a particular office.

The range of functions the Old Testament endowment by the Spirit enabled suggests that the scope of the Spirit's activity is much broader than implied in contemporary discussions of spiritual gifts. The charismatic endowment of the Spirit is thus not restricted to what we commonly regard as 'religious' or 'spiritual' spheres of life. As we have seen, the Spirit who imparted administrative abilities to Moses and Joseph, practical architectural and artistic skills to Bezalel and Oholiab, and military prowess to the judges and military rulers of Israel, is able to gift God's people with corresponding 'secular' skills and the necessary enablement for responsible stewardship of God's creation in the twenty-first century.

The prophetic Spirit

A chief activity of the Spirit all through the history of Israel was manifested in the spirit of prophecy. We observe a further indication of the tendency towards institutionalization of the Spirit in the close relationship between the Spirit's enduring presence and action, and the office of the prophet. In all prophetic activity the Spirit of God acts as the channel of communication between God and the human person. As the Spirit makes God's will and wisdom known to the prophet in a dream, vision or word, the message from the Lord is conveyed by the prophet through an oracular speech or prophecy. God's revelation was thus directly or indirectly traced to the Spirit, and the prophet was regarded primarily as a 'man of the Spirit' (Mic. 3:8; Hos. 9:7).

While there are various ways we could classify the prophets, the most natural categorization is that of the Non-Writing and Writing prophets. The Non-Writing prophets emerged mainly in the earlier history of Israel, so called because while they did have significant ministries, their primary contribution was through the spoken, rather than written, word of prophecy. The best known among them are Elijah and Elisha (1 Kgs 17:1–21:29; 2 Kgs 1:1–13:20), but others, as well as unnamed prophets (1 Kgs 13:1–32), were named too: Nathan (2 Sam. 7:1–17; 12:1–25), Gad (2 Sam. 24:11–25), Ahijah (1 Kgs 11:29–39), Micaiah (1 Kgs 22:8–28) and Azariah (2 Chr. 15:1–7). The Writing prophets who appear later (the eighth century bc onwards) are so called because their spoken prophecies, collected and recorded under their names (Isaiah to Malachi), were eventually included as inspired Scripture within both Hebrew and Christian canons.

The role of the Spirit's empowerment of the prophetic ministry is indicated in the account of the transmission of charismatic power from Elijah to Elisha (2 Kgs 2). The continuous presence of the Spirit of the Lord with Elijah causes the Spirit to be identified here as the 'spirit of Elijah' (2 Kgs 2:9, 15). Elisha's request was for a 'double portion' of the Spirit that was upon Elijah, and through the symbolic action of Elisha taking up Elijah's cloak, the transfer takes place, and is attested by Elisha's use of the cloak to part the waters of the river Jordan miraculously (2 Kgs 2:13–14). There is a clear recognition in this context that the Spirit's presence with the prophet resulted in significant supernatural empowerment (2 Kgs 2:16; cf. 1 Kgs 18:12).

Little is explicitly stated regarding the role of the Spirit in the prophecies of the Writing prophets. Their prophetic utterances are normally prefaced by the expression 'The word of the Lord came to . . .' (Jer. 1:2, 4, 11; Hos. 1:1; Joel 1:1; Zeph. 1:1), without mention of the Spirit's inspiration. Micah is one who clearly asserted the authenticity of his message based on his claim to be 'filled with power, / with the Spirit of the Lord' (Mic. 3:8).

The Spirit appears everywhere in the Writing prophet Ezekiel. The opening vision of his book shows the living creatures full of movement and power: the wheels went wherever the spirit of the creatures within the wheels took them (Ezek. 1:12, 20). The point of the vision appears to have been to emphasize the dynamic and active presence of God's glory among his people in Babylonian captivity (Ezek. 1:22–28). According to Ezekiel's testimony, the Spirit enters and commissions him (Ezek. 2:2; 3:24), lifts him up and carries him away to various locations in a visionary state (Ezek. 2:2; 3:12, 14; 8:3; 11:1, 24; 37:1; 43:5). The Spirit brings God's message to the prophet (Ezek. 2:2), and the Spirit comes upon him and tells him what to speak (Ezek. 11:5).

The Spirit's role in the inspiration of the prophets is also affirmed clearly elsewhere in the Old Testament. Zechariah, a prophet who came after the exile, refers to 'the words that the Lord Almighty had sent by his Spirit through the earlier prophets' (Zech. 7:12). Much later the prayer of penitent confession of the children of Israel that Nehemiah records includes a reference to the Spirit's action through the prophets: 'For many years you [the

Lord] were patient with them. By your Spirit you admonished them through your prophets' (Neh. 9:30).

The Spirit of God revealed divine truth to prophets in a variety of ways: through audible voice, internal impression, vision and supernatural insight. A key issue for the common people was how to distinguish between true prophets, who spoke as God's infallible spokespersons, and *false* (or *presumptuous*) prophets, who claimed to speak for God, but had not actually heard from him (1 Kgs 22:7–22; Jer. 23:9–40).

The criteria given are threefold: (1) A true prophet's predictions must come to pass (Deut. 18:15–22); (2) a true prophet's teaching must be consistent with earlier divine revelation (Deut. 13:1–5), since God will not contradict himself; (3) a true prophet's message must be ethically acceptable. An early illustration of this can be found in the prophet Micah (Mic. 3:5–8). Until this point the Old Testament actions of the Spirit are seen to be ethically neutral. Micah clearly brings in the ethical dimension by linking his empowerment by the Spirit to his ethical message of God's condemnation of the moral corruption and social injustice prevailing in Israel (cf. Isa. 11:2–3; 32:15–17; Ezek. 36:23–31). The prophet's message should be accepted only after it has been tested by these criteria.

In the New Testament, Peter declares that the Old Testament prophetic Scripture 'never had its origin in the will of man, but men spoke from God as they were carried along by the Holy Spirit' (2 Pet. 1:21). Thus not only does he affirm clearly the Holy Spirit as the source of Old Testament prophetic activity; he elsewhere identifies this prophetic Spirit as 'the Spirit of Christ', and the same Holy Spirit through whose enablement the New Testament preachers proclaimed the gospel of Christ (1 Pet. 1:10–12). We thus find a strong element of continuity in the prophetic activity of the Spirit in the Old and New Testaments.

The messianic Spirit

We find a strand within the Old Testament prophetic tradition of the future expectation of a universal outpouring of the Spirit, closely associated with a coming ideal king, the Messiah or Anointed One, upon whom the Spirit would rest in mighty power. This messianic hope was grounded originally in the Spirit's empowerment of king David and the royal line, regarded as the channel of God's blessings upon his people. Dissatisfaction with earthly kings led eventually to aspirations for a future ideal king of the line of David, who would be uniquely endowed with the Spirit to usher in a perfect age.

The clearest predictions concerning this ideal king and his perfect rule are in Isaiah. His earthly descent from David and his strong endowment of the Spirit are described in Isaiah 11:1–2:

> A shoot will come up from the stump of Jesse;
>> from his roots a Branch will bear fruit.
> The Spirit of the Lord will rest on him –
>> the Spirit of wisdom and of understanding,
>> the Spirit of counsel and of power,
>> the Spirit of knowledge and of the fear of the Lord.

The following verses go on to describe his compassionate and righteous rule and the perfect quality of life experienced as a consequence (Isa. 11:3–9).

In one of the 'Servant' passages that clearly points to the coming Messiah, Isaiah records:

> Here is my servant, whom I uphold,
>> my chosen one in whom I delight;
> I will put my Spirit on him
>> and he will bring justice to the nations.
> (Isa. 42:1)

As a result of the Spirit's bestowal, the Messiah will be endowed with justice, humility, gentleness, faithfulness and patience (Isa. 42:2–4). These words are quoted in the New Testament in the context of Jesus' compassionate healing of many sick people (Matt. 12:18–21). Another passage asserts that the coming Messiah will be anointed by the Spirit of God in order to fulfil his mission:

> The Spirit of the Sovereign Lord is on me,
>> because the Lord has anointed me
>> to preach good news to the poor.
> He has sent me to bind up the brokenhearted,
>> to proclaim freedom for the captives
>> and release from darkness for the prisoners,
> to proclaim the year of the Lord's favour . . .
> (Isa. 61:1–2)

Jesus read from this passage when he inaugurated his ministry at Nazareth, claiming it was being fulfilled in himself on that day, in the presence of his hearers (Luke 4:16–19, 21).

The really distinctive aspect of the future blessings of the Spirit, however, is that the Spirit will no longer be the monopoly of a few people: judges, kings, prophets and others assigned specific tasks. Both Isaiah and Ezekiel speak of a widespread bestowal of the Spirit (Isa. 44:3; Ezek. 39:29), but the awesome disclosure is given by Joel in his prediction that there will come a time when the Spirit will be available to all:

> And afterwards,
>   I will pour out my Spirit on all people . . .
> (Joel 2:28)

Towards the end of the Old Testament period a belief arose that the Spirit had been withdrawn from Israel until the Messiah arrived. The expectation of a future universal outpouring thus became more closely associated with the coming messianic age. This widespread outpouring would not only be accompanied by charismatic manifestations (Joel 2:28–32), but also lead to purification from sin and deep spiritual renewal in Israel (Ezek. 37; cf. Hag. 2:5; Zech. 4:6; 12:10), and result in the re-creation of the hearts of human beings (Jer. 31:31–40; Isa. 59:21; Ezek. 36:25–27). This is in keeping with our understanding of the Spirit of God as the action of God that creates new life – a sanctifying and transforming function of the Spirit only fully clarified and fulfilled in the New Testament era with the coming of Christ.

The promise fulfilled

This was then the hope, the promise, given to Israel and through Israel to the world. When we turn to the New Testament, we are confronted with the testimony of the earliest disciples of Jesus, who were convinced that the promised outpouring of the Spirit had occurred, and that they had witnessed the beginnings of this fulfilment in their own experience. Consequently, in the Acts of the Apostles, which records the experience of the earliest church, the Spirit is everywhere. The early Christian community was clearly convinced that the Spirit was permanently present with and in them. This conviction was based not only on the Pentecost event (Acts 2), but also on the experiences of the Spirit of growing numbers of communities and individuals that accompanied the spread of the gospel (Acts 8:14–17; 10:44–46; 19:1–6; 1 Cor. 2:4; Gal. 3:5).

This is the basis for the Holy Spirit being described sometimes as the 'eschatological Spirit'. In the Jewish tradition, the gift of the Spirit was a crucial sign of the end of the age. The bestowal of the Spirit upon the earliest Jewish Christians thus clearly indicated that the messianic age had already arrived: 'the Spirit was both the *certain evidence* that the future had dawned, and the *absolute guarantee* of its final consummation' (Fee 1994: 806; italics his). This is captured vividly in three Pauline metaphors of the Spirit: *down payment* (2 Cor. 1:21–22; 5:5; Eph. 1:14), *first fruits* (Rom. 8:23) and *seal* (2 Cor. 1:21–22; Eph. 1:13; 4:30). The presence of the Spirit as an experienced reality among the people of God is both evidence that 'the promise of the Father' has been fulfilled and validation of the claim that the future age has already broken into the present.

The Christian experience of the Holy Spirit thus cannot be viewed in isolation. The first-century Christians claimed their experience of the Spirit was in direct continuity with and fulfilment of the Old Testament promise of a universal bestowal of the Spirit. Their experience of the Spirit as recorded in the New Testament will serve as the normative guide for our reflection on the Spirit's person and work.

4

The Spirit of the Living God

The Spirit as God's Personal Presence

I would like to invite all of you to get on the Holy Ground with me by taking off your shoes while we are dancing to prepare the way of the spirit. With humble heart and body, let us listen to the cries of creation and the cries of the Spirit within it.

Come. The spirit of Hagar, Egyptian, black slave woman exploited and abandoned by Abraham and Sarah, the ancestors of our faith.

Come. The spirit of Uriah, loyal soldier sent and killed in the battlefield by the great King David out of the King's greed for his wife, Bathsheba . . .

Come. The spirit of male babies killed by the soldiers of King Herod upon Jesus' birth.

Come. The spirit of Joan of Arc, and of the many other women burnt at the 'witch trials' throughout the medieval era . . .

Come. The spirit of indigenous people of the earth, victims of genocide during the time of colonialism and the period of great Christian mission to the pagan world.

Come. The spirit of Jewish people killed in the gas chambers during the Holocaust.

Come. The spirit of people killed in Hiroshima and Nagasaki by atom bombs . . .

Come. The spirit of Mahatma Gandhi, Steve Biko, Martin Luther King, Jr., Malcolm X, Victor Jara, Oscar Romero and many

unnamed women freedom fighters who died in the struggle for
liberation of their people . . .

Come. The spirit of the Amazon rainforest now being
murdered every day.

Come. The spirit of Earth, Air and Water, raped, tortured
and exploited by human greed for money . . .

Come. The spirit of the Liberator, our brother Jesus,
tortured and killed on the cross.

The location was Canberra, Australia, the year 1991, the event the Seventh
Assembly of the World Council of Churches, the theme 'Come Holy Spirit,
Renew the Whole Creation', the speaker Chung Hyun-Kyung, a young
South Korean theologian. Her prayer was followed by these opening
explanatory remarks:

I came from Korea, the land of spirits full of *Han. Han* is anger.
Han is resentment. *Han* is bitterness. *Han* is grief. *Han* is broken-
heartedness and the raw energy for struggle for liberation. In my
tradition people who were killed or died unjustly became wandering
spirits, the *Han*-ridden spirits. They are all over the place seeking
the chance to make the wrong right. Therefore the living people's
responsibility is to listen to the voices of the *Han*-ridden spirits and
to participate in the spirits' work of making the right wrong. These
Han-ridden spirits in our people's history have been agents through
whom the Holy Spirit has spoken her compassion and wisdom for
life. Without hearing the cries of these spirits we cannot hear the
voice of the Holy Spirit. I hope the presence of all our ancestors'
spirits here with us shall not make you uncomfortable. For us they
are icons of the Holy Spirit who became tangible and visible to us.
Because of them we can feel, touch and taste the concrete bodily
historical presence of the Holy Spirit in our midst. From my people's
land full of *Han*-filled spirits I came to join with you in another land
of spirits full of *Han*, full of the spirits of the indigenous people,
victims of genocide. (Quoted in King 1994: 392–394)

Until recently it was safe to stereotype people in the West as generally
ignorant concerning matters of 'spirit(s)', while those in the East were
regarded as more at home in the paranormal world of 'spirit(s)'. This is no

longer the case. It is still true that in some parts of the world, traditions of spirituality are deeper and more pervasive. For instance, Sanskrit, the religious and philosophical language of India, is rich with 'spirit' language, and in general people in India very naturally tend to think of life in terms of unseen 'spirit' realities. The same is true of parts of the world shaped by the world views of Eastern religions, folk Islam, African traditional religions and other indigenous religions of aboriginal peoples. We are, however, witnessing a growing surge of interest in spirituality in the West today. Taoism, Tibetan and Zen Buddhism, Spiritualism, Kabbalism, Yoga, New Age spirituality and other forms of Eastern mysticism are all an integral part of Western culture today. People in our world are thus perhaps more aware and accepting of the realm of the spirits today than ever before in recent history.

This offers both great possibilities and pitfalls for our presentation of the biblical notion of Spirit. Chung Hyun-Kyung's invocation of various *Han*-ridden spirits based on her conviction that they mediated the presence of the Holy Spirit illustrates the most serious danger: syncretism. How does Chung Hyun-Kyung so readily and audaciously link the Holy Spirit with *Han*-ridden spirits of 'the indigenous people, victims of genocide'? Likewise, the monistic overtones of her identification of the Spirit with the natural elements are unmistakable. Chung Hyun-Kyung's sensational presentation illustrates graphically that in the realm of mystical spiritual experience the borders between different faiths become indistinct and hazy as truth claims become subordinate to subjective preferences.

My primary concern in this and the following chapters is to clarify the biblical account of the Holy Spirit in the context of myriad prevailing conceptions of 'spirit', some of which overlap, while others compete with the biblical notion. How does the Christian understanding of the Holy Spirit relate to other ideas of spirit, such as Brahman in Hinduism or 'the Force' in *Star Wars*? Is the Holy Spirit to be viewed essentially in personal terms, or must we look beyond the personalist language and regard the Spirit as in fact an impersonal, abstract force? Is it all right to affirm, with most Eastern religions, the essential identity of the human with the divine spirit, and blur the distinction between the two as Chung Hyun-Kyung does self-assuredly? Is the Holy Spirit God? If so, in what sense, and how does his divinity relate to that of the Father and Jesus?

The Holy Spirit as person

The Holy Spirit is unlike anything we know. The titles 'Father' and 'Son' convey the idea of personhood naturally, whereas we normally tend to think of 'Holy Spirit' in impersonal terms. The Hebrew (*rûah*) and Greek (*pneuma*) terms for 'Spirit' mean 'breath' or 'wind', both impersonal concepts, and the common images for spirit (oil, fire, water) seem to suggest an impersonal force. Several passages in the New Testament in fact seem to treat the Holy Spirit impersonally, in language that suggests he is a dynamic force or a fluid-like effluence rather than a person.

The Spirit is thus able to 'fill' a person (Luke 4:1; Acts 2:4), be 'poured out' like fluid (Rom. 5:5; Titus 3:6), and granted as a gift (Luke 11:13). The use of the genitive ('of ') sometimes suggests that the Spirit can be partaken of in shares or portions, incompatible with the notion of personhood (Acts 2:18; Heb. 6:4). John the Baptist's predictions concerning the baptism with the Spirit omit the definite article in relation to the Spirit and compare it with water baptism, more appropriately denoting that the Spirit is a fluid-like effluence rather than a person (Matt. 3:11; Mark 1:8; Luke 3:16). Jesus' post-resurrection pronouncement to his disciples 'Receive Holy Spirit' likewise omits the definite article (John 20:22) with the same implication. Some regard the frequent absence of the definite article in references to the Spirit as also undermining the idea of personhood (Acts 18:25; Rom. 12:11; 14:17; 1 Cor. 12:3; 14:16) (Wainwright 1962: 202; Plantinga 1988: 916).

The Christian belief in the Holy Spirit was formulated within the context of a belief in the existence of spirits, good and evil, which have distinct personal identities. Given this background, the impersonalist language is inconclusive, especially when we consider all of the New Testament evidence (Fee 1994: 15–24). The New Testament presents convincing reasons for believing that Jesus and the early Christians clearly thought of the Holy Spirit in personal terms.

1. *The Spirit as 'Paraclete'*: This is a title John especially likes: 'And I will ask the Father, and he will give you another Counsellor (*paraklētos*) to be with you for ever – the Spirit of truth' (John 14:16; cf. 14:25; 15:26; 16:7). There is no adequate English translation for the term, which is also variously rendered Comforter, Helper, Advocate or Friend. The word 'another' before Paraclete implies that Jesus thought of himself as the original Paraclete, and the Holy Spirit as his counterpart or 'alter-ego'. The Holy Spirit could thus be 'another' Paraclete, only if he were also a person like Jesus.

The point is underlined by John's distinctive use of the personal pronoun to refer to the Holy Spirit in this context. Where the Spirit is first introduced in John 14:17, John uses the more grammatically correct neuter pronoun 'it' (*ekeino*) when referring to the 'Spirit' (*pneuma*), a neuter noun. Subsequently, however, he repeatedly employs the masculine pronoun 'he' (*ekeinos*) to refer to the Spirit (John 14:26; 15:26; 16:8, 13, 14), although he should more accurately use the neuter pronoun. John clearly wants his readers to view the Holy Spirit as 'he' and not 'it'.

In the context of his teaching on the Paraclete, John ascribes several personal activities to the Spirit. He *teaches* and *reminds* (14:26); *testifies* (15:26); *guides, speaks* and *hears* (16:13); *brings glory to* and *reveals truths about Jesus* (16:14). John's description of the Spirit thus offers unambiguous and substantial proof concerning the Spirit's personhood.

2. *Other sayings of Jesus:* Mark 3:20–30 (cf. Matt. 12:22–32) records Jesus' explanation of the power encounter between Beelzebub (Satan) and the Holy Spirit at work in his ministry. Beelzebub was clearly regarded as a 'he' spirit; hence his opponent, the Holy Spirit, must, likewise, have been regarded as a person. Jesus' warning regarding blasphemy against the Holy Spirit in this context further confirms that he must have conceived of the Holy Spirit as a person (Mark 3:29; Matt. 12:31; cf. Luke 12:10).

In another context, Jesus told his disciples not to be anxious about what to say when they were arrested and brought to trial (Mark 13:11; cf. Matt. 10:20; Luke 12:12). His assurance that the Holy Spirit would speak through them indicates that he regarded the Spirit as a conscious personal agent.

3. *The 'acts' of the Holy Spirit:* The actions of the Spirit recorded in the book of Acts are all of a personal nature. The Holy Spirit *speaks* (1:16; 8:29; 10:19; 11:12; 13:2; 28:25), *witnesses* (5:32); *encourages* (9:31), *approves* (15:28), *sends* (13:4), *guides* (16:6–7), *warns* (20:23), *appoints* (20:28), *can be lied to* and *tested* (5:3, 9) and *can be resisted* (7:51). These activities are appropriately ascribed only to a person.

4. *Paul's teaching:* In Paul's writings, the Spirit is the subject of a large number of verbs that require a personal agent. The Holy Spirit *indwells* (Rom. 8:11; 1 Cor. 3:16; 2 Tim. 1:14), *leads* (Rom. 8:14; Gal. 5:18), *bears witness* (Rom. 8:16), *helps* and *intercedes* (Rom. 8:26), *loves* (Rom. 15:30), *searches* (1 Cor. 2:10), *knows* (1 Cor. 2:11), *teaches* (1 Cor. 2:13), *distributes gifts as he chooses* (1 Cor. 12:11), *gives life* (2 Cor. 3:6), *cries out* (Gal. 4:6), *strengthens* (Eph. 3:16) and *is grieved* (Eph. 4:30). Paul's descriptions of the Spirit's work

confirm further that he is a person rather than an impersonal influence or power.

5. *Other New Testament writings:* The allusions to the Spirit's personhood in other New Testament writings relate most commonly to the Spirit's speaking: in the *Old Testament* (Heb. 3:7), to the *church* (Rev. 2:7, 11, 17, 29; 3:6, 13, 22), *warning of false teaching* (1 Tim. 4:1), *predicting the future* (1 Pet. 1:11), and *in heaven* (Rev. 14:13).

It is thus fair to conclude that although the New Testament writers use impersonal language freely in describing certain aspects of the Spirit's work, they take care to affirm his essential personhood wherever appropriate. The New Testament uses personalist language of the Spirit not just figuratively, but in the fullest sense clearly regards the Spirit as a person, a conscious personal agent.

Two important issues arise from our conclusion concerning the Spirit's full personhood. If the Holy Spirit is a person, how are we to understand his identity in relation to God the Father and Jesus? Is the Holy Spirit God? If so, is he God in the same sense as God the Father? How are we to understand his deity or 'Godness' in relation to God the Father and Jesus? We begin with the prior question regarding the Spirit: *In what sense, if at all, can we speak of the Holy Spirit as God?*

The Holy Spirit as God

The New Testament writers generally assumed the deity of the Spirit, since they clearly regarded it as affirmed in the Old Testament. The real questions for these writers were

- Who is this unique person, Jesus of Nazareth?
- If it is appropriate to speak of him as God, is he then to be identified with the Father?
- Where does the Spirit of God fit into this divine scheme?
- In what sense can we continue to speak of the Spirit as God?

But although the Spirit's deity was never seriously in question, the New Testament does provide us with adequate confirmation of his full deity.

1. *Close association with God, the Father and Jesus, the Son:* A number of New Testament 'triadic' passages refer to the Holy Spirit in close relation to the Father and Son. Perhaps the best known of these is the 'triadic' baptismal formula in Matthew 28:19: 'Therefore go and make disciples of all nations,

baptizing them in the name of the Father and of the Son and of the Holy Spirit'. The singular 'name' of God into which his disciples are to be baptized is a tripersonal name, emphasizing the unity of the three persons. A similar formula is found in Paul's benediction in 2 Corinthians 13:14, 'May the grace of the Lord Jesus Christ, and the love of God, and the fellowship of the Holy Spirit be with you all', and in various other forms elsewhere in the New Testament (Rom. 14:17–18; 1 Cor. 12:4–6; 2 Cor. 1:21–22; Gal. 4:6; Eph. 2:18; 3:14–17; 4:4–6; 2 Thess. 2:13–14; 1 Pet. 1:2). The New Testament authors must have regarded the Holy Spirit in the same terms as they did the Father and Christ. They could not have ascribed deity to them and not to the Holy Spirit.

2. *Jesus recognized the Spirit's deity:* In responding to the Pharisees' accusation that he was driving out demons by the power of Beelzebub (Satan), Jesus warns about the danger of blaspheming against the Holy Spirit (Matt. 12:31–32; cf. Mark 3:28–29). In the New Testament, the sin of blasphemy is normally an act of verbally wounding a divine person. Jesus indicates that blasphemy against the Spirit is much more serious than blasphemy against himself. If we affirm the deity of Jesus, the Holy Spirit cannot be ascribed anything less.

Jesus refers to the Spirit as 'another' (*allos*) Counsellor in John 14:16. The term *allos* signifies another *of the same kind*, suggesting that Jesus ascribed the same status to the Spirit as he did to himself. We thus cannot believe that Jesus is God without accepting the Holy Spirit's deity as well.

3. *The Holy Spirit called 'God':* In rebuking Ananias and Sapphira for misrepresentation and attempting to deceive when bringing their offering to God, Peter asks Ananias why he has lied to the Holy Spirit, and declares, 'You have not lied to men but to God' (Acts 5:4). This is perhaps the only instance in the New Testament where the Holy Spirit is explicitly referred to as 'God'. However, in 1 Corinthians we observe an instance when 'God' and 'Holy Spirit' are used interchangeably. In 1 Corinthians 3:16, Paul asks, 'Don't you know that you yourselves are God's temple and that God's Spirit lives in you?' The indwelling Spirit makes us God's temple, but 'God's temple' is described as the 'temple of the Holy Spirit' again in 1 Corinthians 6:19. To be indwelt by the Holy Spirit thus clearly means to be inhabited by God.

4. *God's words in the Old Testament ascribed to the Holy Spirit in the New Testament:* In two places the writer of Hebrews introduces quotations from the Old Testament with the phrases 'So, as the Holy Spirit says' (Heb. 3:7) and 'The Holy Spirit also testifies . . .' (Heb. 10:15). In the first instance he quotes from Psalm 95:7–11, and in the second from Jeremiah 31:33. The New

Testament authors all had a high view of the inspiration of the Old Testament writings, regarding them as the utterance of God himself. This ascription of the Old Testament words of God to the Holy Spirit clearly confirms that they regarded the Holy Spirit as God.

5. *Divine attributes of the Holy Spirit:* Jesus and the apostles ascribed certain divine attributes to the Holy Spirit. Jesus implied that the Spirit was eternal when he said that the Paraclete would 'be with you for ever' (John 14:16). Hebrews refers to him as 'the eternal Spirit' (Heb. 9:14). The Spirit's unique knowledge of the thoughts of God demonstrates that he is all-knowing (1 Cor. 2:10–11). He has power to raise from the dead in a way only God can, indicating that he is all-powerful (Rom. 1:4; 8:11; Eph. 1:17–20).

6. *Divine activities:* Jesus and the apostles credited the Holy Spirit with many distinctively divine functions: *judgment* (John 16:8–11), *bestowing God's love* (Rom. 5:5), *life-giving* (Rom. 8:11) and *inspiration of God's Word* (2 Pet. 1:21).

We have thus seen that the New Testament teaches that the Holy Spirit is a person who is God. Our belief in the Holy Spirit's distinct divine personhood has profound consequences for our view of God, which we need to explore. We begin by looking more closely at the Spirit's relationship to Jesus.

The Holy Spirit and Christ

The Christian understanding of God is decisively shaped by the Christ-event and its significance. Just as God, the creator of the universe, is known as 'the Father of our Lord Jesus Christ' (2 Cor. 1:3; Eph. 1:3; 1 Pet. 1:3), the Spirit is likewise called 'the Spirit of [Jesus] Christ' (Rom. 8:9; Phil. 1:19). Consequently, in the New Testament the identity and activity of the Holy Spirit are always closely linked to the person and work of Jesus. This intimate association between Christ and the Spirit has led some to view the relationship between the two as one of simple identity. The distinction between Christ and the Spirit is, however, clearly presupposed and affirmed in the New Testament. The Spirit's distinctive personal identity is in fact most plainly disclosed in relation to the life and ministry of Christ and the application of his finished work to the life of the church.

The Gospels constantly emphasize Jesus' role first as the Messiah, the *bearer* of the Holy Spirit, and then as glorified Lord, the sender of the Holy Spirit. The Spirit was active in Jesus' life in the following ways: he *superintended his conception* (Matt. 1:18, 20), *identified him at his baptism* (John 1:32–33), *prepared him through testing* (Luke 4:1–2), *empowered him for his ministry* (Luke 4:14; Acts 10:38), *provided him joyful inspiration* (Luke 10:21), *led him to be crucified* (Heb. 9:14) and *raised him from the dead* (Rom. 1:4; 6:4; 8:11).

The Spirit's bestowal upon humans is clearly linked to the ministry of Jesus (Matt. 3:11; Mark 1:18; Luke 3:16) and, more specifically, to his glorification (John 7:37–39). Peter's speech on the day of Pentecost makes especially clear that the bestowal of the Holy Spirit has been made possible only through the death, resurrection and subsequent glorification of Jesus Christ (Acts 2:22–24): 'God has raised this Jesus to life, and we are all witnesses of the fact. Exalted to the right hand of God, he has received from the Father the promised Holy Spirit and has poured out what you now see and hear' (Acts 2:32–33). The New Testament thus always closely associates the active presence and ministry of the Holy Spirit with the crucified and risen Christ, by whom the Spirit is bestowed (Rom. 8:9–11; 1 Cor. 3:16–17; Gal. 4:6).

The Paraclete sayings of Jesus are especially instructive in this regard. Jesus' reference to the Spirit as 'another Paraclete' (John 14:16) implies that the Spirit would be for his disciples everything Jesus was for them during his earthly ministry. This is underlined in the words that immediately follow: he would not leave them as orphans, but would come back to them (John 14:18). The presence of Jesus after his return to the Father is thus mediated in and through the Holy Spirit. The Spirit's teaching and guidance into truth is a reminder of what Jesus has already taught, and he speaks only what he hears from Jesus (John 14:26; 16:13–14). It is Jesus whom the Spirit will glorify and about whom he will testify (John 16:14; 15:26). At the same time, the Holy Spirit's identity is clearly distinguished: he is *another* Paraclete (John 14:16), who comes from the Father and is sent by Jesus (John 15:26; 16:7).

Paul, too, was clearly convinced that the Spirit is the way the risen Christ is present in the midst of his people. Christ gives definition to the Spirit and prescribes his activity: those who have received the Spirit are God's children, co-heirs with Christ (Rom. 8:14–17); and Christ is the decisive criterion for the true activity of the Spirit (1 Cor. 12:3). Paul's favourite expression for describing a believer is the frequently recurring phrase 'in Christ' (Gal. 2:17); but the believer is also 'in the Spirit' (1 Cor. 6:11). We are sanctified 'in Christ' (1 Cor. 1:2), but also sanctified 'in the Spirit' (1 Cor. 6:11). Those sealed 'in Christ' (Eph. 1:13) are also sealed 'in the Spirit' (Eph. 4:30).

The expressions 'in Christ' and 'in the Spirit' are sometimes thought to be interchangeable (Rom. 8:1, 9; Phil. 2:1), thus supporting the identification of Christ and Spirit. Despite the resemblances, however, the two formulae function quite differently in many instances and are hence not easily interchangeable (Fee 1994: 833, 838). A significant instance of this differentiation is in Romans 8, where verses 26–27 describe the Spirit's work of intercession and verse 34 refers to Christ's intercessory ministry. Despite the seeming identification of function, the distinction could not be clearer. While the Spirit exercises his ministry on earth, interceding from within the lives of believers, the risen Christ is in heaven, making intercession at the right hand of God the Father. Christians are thus called to 'clothe [themselves] with the Lord Jesus Christ' (Rom. 13:14) and 'to be conformed to the likeness of his [God's] Son' (Rom. 8:29), not to put on 'the Spirit' or conform to the image of 'the Spirit'. Likewise, Christ was raised from the dead, and believers are exhorted to die, not with the Spirit but with Christ.

The Holy Spirit is thus active as the agent who effects the finished work of Christ in the life of the believer: he *accompanies the initiation of Christians* (Acts 2:38; 1 Cor. 12:13), *provides inner confirmation of the believer's sonship* (Rom. 8:15; Gal. 4:6), *empowers for witness* (Acts 4:31), *sanctifies* (Rom. 15:16) and *gives life* (2 Cor. 3:6). But although there is a close relationship between Jesus and the Spirit in all these actions, the identity and functions of the two are consistently distinguished.

The biblical teaching on the Spirit's full personhood thus distinguishes the Paraclete clearly from impersonal monistic notions of spirit that control most forms of Eastern and New Age spirituality. The biblical affirmation of the Spirit's full deity also clearly sets him apart from conceptions of spirit where the distinction between the human and divine spirit is glossed over. The notion of 'spirit' observed in the opening paragraphs of this chapter in Chung Hyun-Kyung's Canberra prayer bears no resemblance to the biblical description of the Holy Spirit. The monism implied in her invocation of the 'spirit' within creation, the Amazon rainforest and Earth, Air and Water is foreign to the biblical representation of the Spirit. So also is her identification of this immanent creation-'spirit' with the 'spirits' of various oppressed figures in the Bible and down through history. The decisive departure from biblical teaching is in her blatant failure to affirm any distinction between these various 'spirits' and the 'Spirit' of Jesus himself.

Chung Hyun-Kyung's notion of 'spirit' is thus more akin to *shamanism* than to the biblical description of the Holy Spirit, made explicit in her explanatory remarks drawing attention to 'the presence of all our ancestors' spirits here with us'. For her, these 'ancestor-spirits' are 'agents' and 'icons' of the Holy Spirit, which mediate the 'concrete bodily historical presence of the Holy Spirit', and without whom 'we cannot hear the voice of the Holy Spirit'. From the perspective of biblical Christianity this is serious error, even blasphemous heresy, reminding us of John's warning 'Do not believe every spirit, but test the spirits to see whether they are from God . . .' (1 John 4:1).

A biblically informed understanding of the Spirit's true identity is thus critical if we are to exercise the spiritual gift of 'discerning of spirits' (1 Cor. 12:10) effectively today. The Holy Spirit must not be confused with any other spirit: a general spiritual immanence or impersonal divine influence, a human spirit or some other supernatural spiritual being. He is the transcendent *Holy Spirit*, distinct and separate from his creation. He is the Spirit *of God* and *of Christ*, the personal presence of God himself. The church, corporately and individually, is the locus of God's personal presence, and the Spirit is the way God is now present with his people. His role is to make the personal presence of God and fellowship with Christ experienced realities in the lives of his followers. The ultimate purpose of the Holy Spirit's ministry is to mediate the presence of the risen Lord Jesus Christ. Everything the Spirit does is directed towards creating and deepening an awareness of the reality of Jesus in human experience (Packer 2005: 49–50, 56–58). A clearer picture of the Spirit's divine personhood will emerge as we consider the biblical teaching concerning his relation to God the Father and our Lord Jesus Christ in the following chapter.

5

The Two Hands of God

The Spirit and the Trinity

His tone was intense and confident, even condescending: 'I told them you are confused about the Trinity because you don't know your Bible. The Bible teaches that the Father is God . . . Jesus is not God: he is the Son of God. Neither is the Holy Spirit God: it is just the Spirit or power of God. If you read your Bible more you would know that!' My friend was sharing his response to his nominal Christian family members who were ridiculing his recent experience of spiritual renewal by raising questions on the seeming absurdity of the doctrine of the Trinity. We were all relatively new believers, but after having completed one year of Bible college, I was slightly better informed and thus horrified: 'Ravi, do you realize that what you just stated and defended so vehemently to your family members sounds more like Jehovah's Witness teaching than biblical Christianity!' My friend Ravi was a fine believer, who had recently given his life to Christ, and genuinely desired to follow Christ and live for him. Ravi is, however, typical of many Christians for whom the doctrine of God as Trinity is at best a fuzzy, meaningless notion, and at worst a dreadful embarrassment.

We have seen that the New Testament Christians were convinced that the Spirit is God, and that he is a person, distinct from the Father and Jesus, the Son. This should raise questions in our minds as it did for the earliest followers of Jesus, as they tried to reconcile the strict Jewish monotheism of their forefathers with this understanding of God as Father, Son and Holy Spirit. If Jesus was God, and the Spirit is regarded as not just a divine force but a God-person, can we still continue to speak of God as *one*? Is God one person or three? If we maintain that Father, Jesus and the Spirit are *three* distinct persons, then how can Christians still claim to believe in *one* God? No wonder those outside the church, and frequently Christians themselves, find the notion of the Trinity, a 'three-in-one' God, confusing and a logical contradiction.

A proper conception of the Trinity is crucial for a sound understanding of the Spirit's personhood and full deity. It is not enough to affirm that the Spirit is a person and that he is God. Some explanation is called for concerning how this affirmation fits with the biblical facts relative to God's nature and identity as God, the Father of our Lord Jesus, and his self-disclosure in his Son, Jesus Christ. This is not just an abstract theological issue of concern only to professional theologians, but one that has important bearing on how we interpret the biblical teaching concerning the Spirit's nature and work, as well as the church's devotional practice and social witness.

The Spirit as divine person

Although the Bible gives us neither the term 'Trinity' nor a systematic formulation of the doctrine, its basis is clearly laid out in the New Testament. Scripture affirms that God is one, and presents Jesus Christ as God, a person distinct from God the Father, and the Holy Spirit also as a divine person, distinct from both. The doctrine of the Trinity thus offers the most coherent explanation of the claims and observations surrounding the event of the incarnation as presented to us in the New Testament. The early church summarized the biblical data in the words of the Athanasian Creed as follows: 'So the Father is God, the Son is God, and the Holy Spirit is God; and yet they are not three gods, but one God' (quoted in Plantinga 1988: 914).

The problem from the earliest stages of the doctrine's formulation was how to state the 'threeness' and 'oneness' in terms that accurately reflect the witness of Scripture and yet do not appear logically absurd. There are two alternative directions along which logical reflection on the issue can proceed naturally. One option is to dilute and redefine the three-personhood notion in a way that preserves a strict Jewish undifferentiated monotheism. The other is to revise the conception of oneness to accommodate a more explicit assertion of three persons within the Godhead. Consequently, throughout the history of the church, discussion on the role of the Holy Spirit in the Trinity has tended to proceed along these two lines. Generally speaking, the Eastern church has preferred to begin with the tri-personhood of Father, Son and Holy Spirit and to explain the oneness theologically. The Western church, on the other hand, has favoured affirming the undifferentiated unity of God in absolute monotheistic terms first, and then offering justification for the threefold differentiation within the Godhead.

Three persons united in one God-essence, or one God-person in three roles or modes of being? Does it really matter? What difference does it make? There is much in common in the 'centrist' or moderate views held by good evangelicals on both sides of the discussion. However, both approaches have their extreme expressions – the danger of tritheism (belief in three gods), on one hand, and Spirit-monism (belief in only one essential reality: Spirit), on the other. Contemporary expressions of tritheism are relatively rare. There are, however, widespread indications of the growing influence of Spirit-monism within some circles of contemporary theology as well as popular Christian spirituality. Some of this is a carry over from nineteenth-century Neoplatonic idealism, but due more to the influence of Eastern monistic spirituality as well as doctrinal errors within many twentieth-century Spirit movements. In seeking to accommodate the biblical view to prevailing philosophical and religious conceptions of 'spirit', some find it convenient to subsume the identities of the Father and Son under that of the Holy Spirit within a simple monistic view of 'Spirit/spirit'.

For many years I failed to appreciate fully the value and relevance of these trinitarian questions to the church's worship and witness until, as a young pastor, I was summoned to respond to a situation faced by a new convert contemplating baptism in our church. An acquaintance had introduced him to the teaching of some 'Oneness' Pentecostals, which had left him confused. My pastoral colleague and I arrived at the home of this new convert for a brief discussion, only to walk into a group of about twenty members of this sect. We were then subjected to a one-hour monologue by the leader of the group who set forth their claim to have received special revelation into the 'mystery' of the Godhead, summarized in the slogan 'Jesus is the Father, Jesus is the Son, Jesus is the Holy Spirit'. When we were finally allowed to get a word in, my colleague and I turned their attention to some of the standard trinitarian formula texts, such as Matthew 28:19 and 2 Corinthians 13:14, but met with little success. Our efforts were countered with patronizing smiles, and our proof-texts dismissed with the claim that 'Father', 'Son' and 'Holy Spirit' in these texts were merely titles describing the different functions of one and the same person – the Lord Jesus Christ.

Then suddenly the light dawned. We told them we would pose just one question, after which we would consider the discussion closed and leave, but they should reflect carefully on their response before offering it. I asked, 'Within the man Jesus Christ were there two persons or one person?' With a confident, knowing smile the leader said, 'That's easy . . . one person of course . . . the Father! We responded, 'So if the one person in Jesus is the Father, every time Jesus speaks it is the Father who speaks . . . is that right?' The leader's response: 'Yes, yes . . . that is what I have been saying all along!' It was what my friend called an 'open goal', and we could not pass the opportunity to score: 'Who is the Father then talking to in Jesus' high priestly prayer in John 17? Each time he refers to "I and the Father . . ." who is "I" and who is "the Father"?' For a while there was chaos in the opposite camp, and then a request to retract: 'Sorry, we misunderstood your question. There were two persons in Jesus: the human Jesus and the Father.' My friend and I could hardly believe our ears. We held out our open Bibles and said, 'Do us a favour . . . can you go through the Gospels for us and wherever the words of Jesus are recorded, please show us how you distinguish the words of the Father from the words of the human Jesus!'

I came back from that meeting grateful for my systematic theology teacher, and more alert than ever of the dangers of a weak trinitarian theology. Several decades ago Claude Welch sounded the following note of caution:

> The religion of the Spirit becomes only a deification of the human spirit . . . unless the Spirit be recognised as the Spirit of Christ and of God the Father of Christ – i.e. unless it be the Holy Spirit who proceeds from the Father and the Son. (Welch 1953: 228–229)

The crucial question in our conception of the Spirit is thus not so much *What is the Holy Spirit?* as *Who is Jesus Christ?*

Welch's observation draws attention to a crucial area where modern reflection on the Holy Spirit is particularly vulnerable. The widespread discontent and disillusionment with materialism in the West has resulted in a surge of interest in matters of the 'spirit', and the growth in influence of New Age spirituality and Eastern mysticism. Under this influence the line between the Divine Spirit and human spirit becomes frequently blurred. We must, however, be wary of drawing superficial parallels: popular contemporary notions of 'spirit' must be carefully evaluated against the biblical description of the Spirit.

As we have seen in the previous chapter, when the Bible describes the Holy Spirit, it does not refer to just any spirit or spirituality, to the spirit of man or to a general immanence of God. The Holy Spirit in the New Testament is a distinct and personal divine Spirit, closely associated with the life and ministry of Jesus, and who came subsequently to indwell and empower the church as a consequence of the finished work of Christ. Our understanding of the Holy Spirit's personhood and our conception of the Trinity is thus vitally and indissolubly linked to God's self-revelation in Jesus Christ.

The Spirit of the Father and of Christ

The Spirit's relationship to the Father and Christ has been expressed variously by the church, sometimes in complex theological formulations and creedal statements, and at other times explained with the help of simple images or analogies. One of the earliest of these was the description by the church father Irenaeus of the Word-Christ and the Spirit as the *Two hands of God*. Irenaeus' analogy must be viewed in the context of the early church fathers' struggle to clarify the identity and function of the Holy Spirit, especially in relation to the Father and the Son. One hand of God was the Word-Christ, by whom God had created the world and reigned over it. This Word-Christ, the Son of God, had become flesh for the salvation of all people. Irenaeus was, however, also aware that wherever the Word-Christ was present, the Spirit was also active: at creation, in the incarnation and at the birth of the church. For Irenaeus, there was no Word (either prophetic or incarnate) without the Spirit. God performed his mighty acts by his *two hands* – the Word and the Spirit. The Spirit also realizes the work of the Word-Christ in the church. The picture of the *Two hands of God* thus helped Irenaeus affirm the essential equality of Son and Spirit, and effectively hold their mission together.

Perhaps a more helpful description finding growing acceptance in recent times views the Spirit's relations to the Father and the Son in social terms as members of *the Perfect Family*. This analogy has its roots in Jesus' high priestly prayer in John 17:21–23: 'that all of them may be one, Father, just as you are in me and I am in you. May they also be in us so that the world may believe that you have sent me . . . that they may be one as we are one: I in them and you in me.' In this final prayer of Jesus for the believing community, we see that although Jesus and the Father are distinct persons, they are 'one' because they are 'in' each other. He prays for the same *oneness* that he and his Father experience within *the Perfect Family* in heaven to be extended to his family on earth, in the disciples' union with the triune God and their relationship to one another. Just as the church, God's family on earth, consists of many members but is still one church, so also God, *the Perfect Family* in heaven, is three persons and yet one.

God is thus conceived of not in terms of a single self, but rather as a community or society of three persons, each of whom is vitally attached to the others in a relationship of mutuality and divine love. The fact that the Trinity is a heavenly or holy family of three members does not imply they are three members of a divine pantheon or independent individual deities. The New Testament emphasizes that the Son is the Son of the Father, and the Spirit is the Spirit of God and of Christ. The Trinity is thus a 'community of being' in whom each person maintains individual identity, but simultaneously shares in the life of the others.

We must be careful to clarify that when we speak of God as three 'persons', we speak of him as personal only in the sense that we humans conceive of personhood. God is ultimately above and beyond all the finite categories that limit our human conceptions of him. What we may safely conclude is that the Holy Spirit is a 'person' in the same sense as the Father and Son are 'persons': a self-conscious subject, distinct from and co-equal to Father and Son.

The Spirit's personal relations

This understanding of the Holy Spirit's personhood has huge implications for the church's faith and practice. To begin with, this view sets apart the Christian conception of Spirit from all other notions of 'spirit', especially as prevalent in various forms of Eastern mystical spirituality. In the quest for a 'pluralistic theology' that would bring together all religions, a growing number of modern theologians are urging that 'God' be recognized as the only absolute, and all religions be regarded as relative. The term 'God' is used in its widest sense to include any and every conception of the ultimate reality or Absolute, which some refer to agnostically simply as 'Mystery'. While various proponents of this broad view have their own distinctive emphases, many believe that the meeting point of all religions is to be found in a common experience of God as 'spirit', which thus provides a meaningful basis for unity among world religions.

The desire for a sympathetic understanding of the religious experience of people of other faiths is to be commended and, as we shall see in a subsequent chapter, is an important prerequisite to effective Christian witness. However, any attempt to engage with non-Christian spiritual experience without reference to the self-revelation of God in Christ must be rejected as inherently flawed. For the believer, nurtured in the teaching of the New Testament, the Spirit is inherently and indisputably a *Person*. Her understanding of the Spirit's personal identity and function is integrally related to the distinctive Christian view of God as Trinity, derived from and dependent on God's self-revelation in Christ.

Perhaps the most important practical implication of this distinctive Christian view of the Spirit is the realization that the Holy Spirit is someone who can be worshipped and to whom we can pray. Confusion about the Trinity, however, frequently results in a devotional dilemma: *Should we pray to and worship the Father, Son, and Holy Spirit separately or together? Or, should prayer and worship be directed to the Father only, or to the Son also, but not the Holy Spirit?* On one hand, some insist that the Scripture explicitly teaches that prayer and worship should be offered only to the Father (e.g. the Lord's Prayer in Matt. 6:9–13), and perhaps also to Jesus (Matt. 14:33; 28:17; 1 Cor. 16:22). They point out that there is little or no explicit New Testament textual evidence to support worship of or prayer to the Holy Spirit.

My case for the legitimacy of worship of and prayer to the Holy Spirit rests on one massive New Testament affirmation: *the Holy Spirit is the personal presence of God himself.* He is fully God, and he is a person, like the Father and the Son, the third member of the Trinity. Consequently, if worship and prayer are due to the Father and the Son, worship and prayer to the Holy Spirit must also be appropriate. The Holy Spirit exercises a personal ministry to believers individually, as well as to the people of God corporately. Thus there can be no doubt that he must have a personal relationship with individual believers and with the church as a whole. Is there any other way, then, to relate to and communicate appropriately with a divine person, the personal presence of God, other than through prayer and worship?

So we must pray to the Holy Spirit, especially relative to his distinctive functions in convicting sinners, illuminating and sanctifying believers, and guiding and empowering the church. We should also appreciate and thank him for what he does and worship him for who he is – the gentle yet powerful Comforter, the Spirit of truth, the Lord and Life-giver of the church. Worship and prayer to the Holy Spirit should, however, never be detached from worship and prayer to the triune God, the proper subject of Christian devotion and petition. Whether Father, Son or Holy Spirit is addressed in worship or prayer, we must remember that the three members of the Trinity share one divine life and always work closely together.

My conclusion regarding the Spirit's fully divine, co-equal personhood confirms my earlier observations concerning his distinctive role in mediating the presence of the risen Christ and of the Father. As the personal presence of God himself, he is the agent through whom God works in the life of the individual believer and the church. He makes known the personal presence of God and of Christ as he indwells, purifies and empowers individual believers and equips the church to confront the unbelieving world with the reality of God. This is the ultimate purpose of the Holy Spirit's ministry, functioning as the 'Go-between God', creating awareness, compelling choices and inducing responses to God's truth revealed (Taylor 1972: 22, 212).

While there are many dimensions to the Spirit's work in mediating the personal presence of God, one that most directly flows from his inner life within the Trinity is best captured in the term *koinōnia* (communion). This beautiful word, used eighteen times in the New Testament, is translated variously as 'fellowship', 'communion' or 'sharing', and describes essentially the believing community's participation in the life of the triune God. While this fellowship is rooted in the divine communion within the three Persons of the Godhead, of which we have a glimpse in Jesus' high priestly prayer (John 17:21–23), the Holy Spirit mediates this divine life to the believing community. This becomes the basis for unity and loving relations within the body of believers and for the gospel invitation to be extended to those outside the church (1 John 1:3). As the personal 'Go-between God' the Holy Spirit seeks effectively to reproduce in the church the intimacy and depth of relations that characterize *koinōnia* life within the Trinity.

I shall never forget a personal experience I had many years ago that convinced me beyond all doubt of the reality of *koinōnia*. We were a small group of young and eager, but unchurched, believers, who until that point in time had little else but the Scripture and the Spirit to guide us in our walk with Christ. Most of us came with a dysfunctional past, bound by various addictions, with psychological and emotional hang-ups, and some were from unstable homes. We had all found salvation in Christ and varied but significant degrees of wholeness through life in the Spirit and genuine commitment to the other person's spiritual and emotional healing.

A recent addition to our group, a recent convert whom I had only just begun to regard as a friend, walked into our home one day right in the midst of a major family crisis. The circumstances were such that by the time he arrived I had begun to doubt whether I would ever again see a beloved member of my family who had been missing all day. My friend walked in and, to my amazement and slight embarrassment, grabbed me in a close embrace. Then without warning he began to weep almost uncontrollably. What made this so perplexing was that he did not know me or my family well enough to identify so deeply with our distress. On the other hand, although my heart was burdened and crushed, I had suppressed all emotions and put up a brave, dryeyed front.

Shortly after, our beloved family member returned, and we gave thanks to God for another wonderful testimony of answered prayer. However, in the course of those poignant moments when my friend expressed deep and heartfelt empathy, I had a glimpse of what the koino nia of the Spirit is meant to be – a taste that will remain with me for ever. My friend had entered into a true experience of the triune God's shared life, which the Holy Spirit extends to the believing community. As a result, he was not merely expressing grief at my pain, but was actually sharing my pain, feeling my sorrow, even shedding my tears. This is an understanding that has stayed with me down through the years and an ideal I constantly reach for in my personal experience and in nurturing other believers in the ways of God.

The *koinōnia* of the Spirit is thus not merely an abstract theological concept or mystical notion, but a realized experience in the church's practical appropriation of life in the Spirit, making the church a *community of the Spirit*. The Spirit thus reproduces in the church distinctive marks of *koinōnia*, or the shared life, including acceptance of the other, regardless of gender, race, tribe, caste or nationality (Rom. 15:7; Gal. 3:28); forgiveness and reconciliation (Eph. 2:14–18; 4:32); mutual submission and dependence (Eph. 5:21; 1 Cor. 12:15–21); joy and contentment that result in secure and serving interpersonal relationships (1 John 1:4; Gal. 5:13); and overflowing, self-giving love that binds the community of God's Spirit-people together in perfect unity (Rom. 13:8; Col. 3:14).

The *koinōnia* of the Spirit is, however, not purely a function internal to the life of the church. As we have seen, the gospel of Christ is an invitation to those outside to enter into fellowship with the Father by accepting the Word of life, the Son, Jesus Christ, and so to enter into the fellowship of the believing community (1 John 1:1–3). In his high priestly prayer Jesus makes it clear that the credibility of the church's witness is inextricably connected to the authenticity of the church's *koinōnia*: 'I pray also for those who will believe in me through their message, that all of them may be one . . . *so that the world may believe that you have sent me*' (John 17:20–21; my italics). This is why the church's social witness is so crucial. The Christian social ethic is in fact grounded not in individual scattered biblical texts, important as they are, but in the nature of God as tri-personal, eternally loving and just, and seeking to extend his life of love and justice to his creation. The Holy Spirit is the active agent who seeks to promote God's loving and just rule through the church. He thus endows the church with love, joy and various other virtues and gifts, not merely for adornment but for service: *good works* (Matt. 5:13–16; Eph. 2:9). The church extends the *koinōnia* of the Spirit even as it engages in acts of compassionate service to the poor and marginalized, but also in social justice endeavours that seek to alleviate the causes of evil and injustice in society.

Christian communities that model this authentic *koinōnia* of the Spirit may be found all over the world. One I have witnessed at close quarters is on the outskirts of the city of Mumbai (Bombay), home to the biggest slum and the largest red-light district in Asia. Dev was born a Hindu but found Christ while employed in the Middle East. Following his call to the ministry and a period of preparation in Bible college, Dev felt called to serve the homeless and hurting people living on the streets of Mumbai. Over the last eighteen years Dev and his team have ministered to hundreds of street people. Drug addicts have been picked off the rubbish dumps, sex workers rescued from cages in the red-light district and AIDS patients provided dignity, a caring home and, in some cases, miraculous healing, a consequence of loving care and believing prayer. All of this and more takes place at the 'Village of Hope', a 40-acre campus that houses a 250-member community consisting of dedicated volunteers, a caring staff and hurting people rescued from the streets and ghettos of Mumbai. Every resident here is a *trophy of God's grace*, and many testimonies may be heard as well as first-hand evidence observed of the transforming power of authentic *koinōnia*.

On one occasion not too long ago, volunteers from the Village of Hope had just walked into the AIDS ward of a hospital in Mumbai when they heard the lilting voice of a little girl chanting a lullaby. When they turned in the direction of the voice, they saw a five-year-old girl holding her six-month-old brother in her arms and trying to rock him to sleep. The lullaby she was singing went something like this: 'Don't worry my little brother, I'll take care of you. / Although everyone has abandoned us I will not abandon you. / I'll beg and borrow if I have to, but I'll make sure you don't go hungry. / And God above will take care of us both.' The brave little girl's song encapsulated their story, but veiled the details of the tragedy. The father had abandoned both mother and three children due to the curse of AIDS, and the mother died of AIDS shortly after. Unable to bear the load of responsibility, the older brother had abandoned his two younger siblings, and now Amjad, the six-month-old baby, was dying of AIDS with no one in the world to care for him but his five-year-old sister, Yasmin. The Government hospital had written off both these children as hopeless cases and left them to fend for themselves in an obscure corner of the AIDS ward.

The Village of Hope volunteers had to go through a slow and convoluted process to obtain custody of Yasmin and Amjad, following which they took them into their community. They cared for them and saw that they received proper medical attention and nourishment. Within the environment of authentic *koinōnia*, Yasmin and Amjad felt love, acceptance and a sense of belonging. They entered into the simple devotional life of the community and experienced healing and marvellous transformation. Today, three years after they first entered the Village of Hope, Yasmin and Amjad are still alive and well, enjoying happy, healthy lives – a living testimony to the reality and efficacy of the true *koinōnia* of the Holy Spirit.

The *Two Hands of God* presents us with a simple but vivid picture of the Holy Spirit's identity and relationship to other members of the Trinity. In the next chapter we look more closely at the objective means God has put in place to ensure that the Holy Spirit works closely with the other *Hand of God*, the Word-Christ, about whom the written Word testifies.

6

The Spirit of Truth

The Spirit and the Word

'Have you ever read the Bible? You will find answers to many questions about life as you read it.'

'I have read the Bible through three times so far, but I will read it again.'

I looked at the lady sitting in front of me somewhat at a loss for words. The big vermillion mark in the centre of her forehead gave visible testimony to her identity as a devout follower of a modern Hindu sect. Her story was extraordinary and would elicit deep admiration in any hearer. She had been married for about ten years to a well-placed Government official when tragedy snatched him away. Left with five daughters, including a year-and-a-half toddler, she was forsaken by all her relatives. She had opted not to remarry or seek employment, since there was no one to take care of her children. Her only source of income was a piece of property she had rented out. But over the previous seventeen years she had seen four of her daughters through engineering college and was, in true Indian tradition, gearing up to help all her daughters get married and settled. She completed her story with a flourish, pointing upwards as she declared, 'All through his help . . . I could not have done it without him!'

Her only source of slight unhappiness was her eldest daughter, physically challenged since birth, who had seven years earlier brought shame to the family when she decided to follow Christ. This daughter had just graduated from Bible college and, for the first time in seven years, mother and daughter had a brief reunion, the occasion for the encounter I just described. The lady was personable and pleasant, and after making our acquaintance over two days, agreed to attend a church service with us. We had just returned from the service and I expected her to be full of questions. I was wrong. To our amazement, when I asked her if she had read the Bible, she responded that she had not only read it, but had also been to church a couple of times before. I was taken aback by her answer. The tone of her answer was not defensive, just polite and matter of fact. How many Christians do you know who have read the Bible through three times? I nursed the hopeful possibility that this lady was a secret believer or, perhaps, close to the kingdom, like Cornelius. I was totally unprepared to find out later that just before she left she asked her daughter to consider forsaking her faith in Christ and return home to her mother's religion and way of life.

This incident helped confirm afresh something I already knew to be true: the knowledge of God does not come by human discovery but by divine revelation. The living Jesus Christ does speak to us with life-transforming impact through the Bible, but this does not happen naturally or automatically – only through the revealing work of the Holy Spirit, about whom Jesus promised, 'But when he, the Spirit of truth, comes, he will guide you into all truth' (John 16:13). Without the Spirit the words of Scripture can be lifeless and ineffective; as Paul says, 'the letter kills, but the Spirit gives life' (2 Cor. 3:6). At this point Word and Spirit converge in the work of divine revelation.

The way the Word of God and the Spirit of God work together closely in the plan of God is captured vividly, as we have noted in the previous chapter, in the church father Irenaeus' famous metaphor of the 'Two Hands of God'. Against the Gnostic overemphasis on God's transcendence, effectively denying his creation and control of the universe, Irenaeus insisted God is involved in the world both as Word and Spirit, and, by their combined agency, performs all his mighty acts. For Irenaeus, there was no Word, by the prophet or as the Son, without the Spirit. Irenaeus' conception was firmly grounded in Scripture (Haroutunian 1974: 155–156).

God created the world by the Word and the Spirit (Gen. 1:1–2), and sends his Word by the Spirit through the prophets (Zech. 7:12). It was through the agency of the Spirit that the incarnation of the Word was effected (Luke 1:35; Matt. 1:20). Furthermore, it is through the Spirit and the Word that the work of Christ is realized in the church: acceptance of the gospel is linked vitally to being sealed with the Holy Spirit (Eph. 1:13); being strengthened in our inner being by the Spirit is associated with the indwelling of Christ in our hearts (Eph. 3:16–17); and receiving the Spirit leads to having the mind of Christ (1 Cor. 2:12–16). The Word is quickened by the Spirit, and the Spirit always directs us to the Word.

While Irenaeus mainly had in mind the living Word, Jesus Christ, by inference this applies also to the testimony of the written Word of Scripture. We see this especially in the Reformers' description of the complementary activity of Word and Spirit. Luther, for instance, asserted that 'the Holy Ghost … works in the hearts of whom he will, and how he will, but never without the Word'. Calvin likewise insisted that 'the Word is the instrument by which the Lord dispenses the illumination of his Spirit to believers' (Bloesch 2000: 275).

The Spirit thus superintends the entire process of formulation, preservation and transmission of the Scriptures, as well as their illumination and interpretation to people. While the wide range of the Holy Spirit's work in relation to Scripture includes all these facets variously classified, we shall focus our attention on two critical issues: the Spirit's role in the *authorship of Scripture* and the Spirit's role in the *application of Scripture* to the life of the believing community.

The Holy Spirit and the divine authorship of Scripture

Jesus referred to the Holy Spirit as 'the Spirit of truth', indicating that his task was to lead people into God's truth. The Spirit is not only the channel and facilitator of revelation, but also the source and agent of revelation. As servant and speaker of the Word he magnifies not himself but Jesus Christ. Bloesch says, 'The relation of Word and Spirit is a relation not of cause and effect but of promise and fulfillment. The Spirit brings to fulfillment the promises contained in holy Scripture' (Bloesch 2000: 277). The Spirit thus functions pivotally in making God known – 'revealing' him to humanity.

Revelation is simply the act of making something known that was previously unknown, and divine revelation refers to the acts and means of God's self-disclosure. Theologians commonly distinguish between 'general' revelation and 'special' revelation. 'General' revelation refers to the disclosure of God in nature, history and the moral law within the human heart, available to all people at all times everywhere (Lewis and Demarest 1996: 61). The Spirit's active role in creation suggests that he must ensure that the divine witness in the world accurately and consistently reflects what God intends to reveal about himself. We shall look at this a little more closely when we discuss the Spirit at work in the world. Our immediate concern is with the Spirit's role in 'special' revelation as it relates to the divine authorship of Scripture.

'Special' revelation refers to divine disclosures to specific people at specific times and places, climaxing in God's self-revelation in Christ and recorded by the prophets and apostles in the Bible. In the Old Testament we see God making his will known to people through his Spirit; likewise, in the New Testament era, God makes himself known to people in Christ through the Holy Spirit.

An integral aspect of the Spirit's revealing ministry is what is commonly distinguished as *inspiration*. The word 'inspiration' is commonly used to describe the surge of creative energy that comes to a poet, artist or musician; the motivation that comes for some extraordinary feat of heroism or physical endurance; at other times the stirring of romantic or filial emotions. But the term has a distinctive meaning when applied to Scripture: 'that supernatural influence of the Holy Spirit upon the Scripture writers which rendered their writings an accurate record of the revelation or which resulted in what they wrote actually being the Word of God' (Erickson 1985: 199).

Inspiration is thus a natural extension of the Spirit's function as revealer, and has to do with the recording of revelation in the text of Scripture. Just as the Spirit was active in the process of divine revelation, revealing the mind and will of God to the apostles and prophets, so also he was active in inspiration, sovereignly guiding the authors of Scripture so that they recorded divine revelation exactly as God wanted them to, without addition or omission. So while the Spirit's role in revelation and inspiration can be logically distinguished, they are organically part of the same revealing activity of the Spirit. It is thus theoretically possible that the recipients of revelation did not record in Scripture all that was revealed to them, but inspiration presupposes revelation, so that all of Scripture is equally revealed and inspired, the end product of the revealing activity of the Holy Spirit.

Two New Testament texts provide the primary basis for the Christian belief in the Holy Spirit's inspiration of the Scriptures. First, 'Above all, you must understand that no prophecy of Scripture came about by the prophet's own interpretation. For prophecy never had its origin in the will of man, but men spoke from God as they were carried along by the Holy Spirit' (2 Pet. 1:20–21).

Peter has just finished describing his experience of Jesus on the mount of transfiguration (Matt. 17:5; Mark 9:7; Luke 9:35), but here places the objective revelation of God – the prophetic word – above his personal experience as a more reliable basis for faith. Scripture has its origin not in the will of man but in the will of God. The expression 'carried along' suggests the metaphor of a ship that moves along by the wind in its sails. God thus employed human instruments: 'men spoke', but were controlled sovereignly by the Holy Spirit in what they spoke and recorded in Scripture.

Secondly, 'All Scripture is God-breathed and is useful for teaching, rebuking, correcting and training in righteousness, so that the man of God may be thoroughly equipped for every good work' (2 Tim. 3:16–17).

The key word in this text is the compound word *theopneustos*, translated 'God-breathed', indicating that the Scriptures were written down as they were 'breathed out' by God (perhaps better understood as 'expiration' than 'inspiration'). The combination of the singular noun *graphē* (Scripture) with the distributive adjective *pasa* (all) suggests Paul is asserting that every passage of Scripture is God-breathed.

The 'Scripture' in both these passages, of course, refers originally to the Jewish Scriptures or the Old Testament, since the New Testament as we have it today was not yet in existence. However, the Christian belief that the Spirit inspired people to speak and to write has its roots in the Jewish doctrine of inspiration. The Scriptures were regarded as Spirit-inspired writings, because of which they were ascribed absolute divine authority. What Scripture says was equal to what God says. The church originally received the truth through the testimony of the apostles, and from earliest times believed that the Holy Spirit inspired the apostolic witness. If the Spirit had inspired the Old Testament prophetic words that pointed only in a veiled way to the coming Messiah (Luke 24:44; 1 Pet. 1:10), it was logical to expect that the same Spirit must have inspired the testimony of those who were eyewitnesses of his coming.

The writer of Hebrews sets forth clearly the basis for the Christian belief in the divine authorship of Scripture: 'In the past God spoke to our forefathers through the prophets at many times and in various ways, but in these last days he has spoken to us by his Son . . .' (Heb. 1:1–2). Hebrews asserts that in the Old Testament, God disclosed his will and nature through the prophets, but in his Son, Jesus Christ, God discloses himself. The Old Testament is thus the record of God's Word through the prophets, and the New Testament is the written testimony of God's self-disclosure in Jesus Christ. Although the role of the Spirit is not explicitly mentioned, it is clearly assumed. The Spirit was and is the agent of all communication from God. The giving and receiving of revelation are his work (1 Cor. 2:9–16; 2 Cor. 3:12–4:6; Eph. 1:17; 3:5; 1 John 2:27).

We believe in the divine origin of the Scriptures, that they record the divine revelation given to the prophets and apostles by the Spirit based on the following grounds: the *testimony of Old Testament authors*, the *attitude of*

Jesus and the apostles to the Old Testament, and the *claims of New Testament authors*. We shall look at each of these in turn.

The testimony of Old Testament authors

In chapter 3 we observed that one of the key functions of the Spirit in the Old Testament was to inspire the prophets to speak from God. Moses was commanded to write down the words God gave him (Exod. 34:27; Deut. 31:24–26). David, too, acknowledged the Spirit's control in the words he spoke:

> The Spirit of the Lord spoke through me;
>> his word was on my tongue.
> (2 Sam. 23:2)

The later prophets used a variety of formulas to affirm the divine origin of their spoken and written words: 'The word of the Lord came to . . .' (Ezek. 12:1; Jon. 1:1); 'This is what the Lord says . . .' (Amos 1:3; Hag. 1:5); 'Hear the word of the Lord . . .' (Hos. 4:1).

God instructed Isaiah to record his message in writing (Isa. 8:1), so that it may be 'an everlasting witness' (Isa. 30:8), and he later refers to a prophetic message preserved in 'the scroll of the Lord' (Isa. 34:16). Jeremiah was conscious of speaking words given to him by God (Jer. 1:7–9), and was also commanded to write God's words in a book (Jer. 30:2). The procedure by which his prophecy was put into writing is described in some detail in Jeremiah 36:1–6. Hosea describes God's prophet as an 'inspired man' (Hos. 9:7), and Micah claims to be 'filled with power, with the Spirit of the Lord' (Mic. 3:8). The Old Testament writers thus clearly affirm the divine origin and authority of Scripture.

The attitude of Jesus and the apostles to the Old Testament

Jesus clearly acknowledged the divine authority of the Spirit-inspired prophetic writings. When tempted by Satan, he quoted the Old Testament with the introductory formula 'It is written', implying its final authority (Matt. 4:4, 6–7, 10; cf. Luke 19:46). He insisted that the Law and the Prophets must be fulfilled and believed (Matt. 5:17–18; Luke 24:25). Luke records Jesus as insisting that not even 'the least stroke of a pen' in the law will go without fulfilment (Luke 16:17). Jesus quotes from the Old Testament, describing the words of Moses and Isaiah as the 'commands of God', and accuses the

Pharisees and teachers of the law of trying to nullify the 'word of God' by their human tradition (Mark 7:5–13; Matt. 15:3–9; cf. Isa. 29:13; Exod. 20:12; 21:17). Jesus recognizes the Spirit's inspiration of the Old Testament when, for instance in quoting from Psalm 110:1, he refers to David as speaking 'by the Spirit' (Matt. 22:43–44; Mark 12:36). Jesus thus assumes that the Old Testament is historically, prophetically and doctrinally authoritative (Lewis and Demarest 1996: 141–142).

The apostolic writers, likewise, in keeping with the prevalent Jewish belief, regard the Old Testament as the inspired Word of God. This is reflected in the formulas they use in quoting Old Testament prophecies: 'what the Lord had said through the prophet' (Matt. 1:22; 2:15), and their citation of the Old Testament to justify beliefs through phrases such as 'it is written' (Rom. 1:17; 11:26; Gal. 3:13) or 'the Scripture says' (Rom. 10:11; 1 Tim. 5:18).

They also specifically recognize the Spirit's inspiration of Old Testament authors. Early in Acts, Peter refers to the Holy Spirit's speaking through David regarding the fate of Judas (Acts 1:16, 20); and the prayer of the early church, likewise, mentions God speaking 'by the Holy Spirit through the mouth of . . . David' (Acts 4:25). Paul also recalls the Holy Spirit speaking through the prophet Isaiah (Acts 28:25–26). The writer of Hebrews, too, refers to the 'voice' of the Holy Spirit in Psalm 95 (Heb. 3:7–8), recognizes the Holy Spirit's testimony in the prophecy of Jeremiah (Heb. 10:16–17; cf. Jer. 31:33–34), and even ascribes the detailed descriptions of the tabernacle in the Old Testament to the Holy Spirit's inspiration (Heb. 9:8). Peter recognizes the active presence of the Spirit in the Old Testament prophets as they predicted various details of the life and work of Christ (1 Pet. 1:10–11). The New Testament thus treats the Old Testament as recording the abiding voice of the Spirit.

The claims of New Testament authors

The New Testament, too, claims to be of divine origin. We see evidence of this especially in Paul's writings. Paul claims to have Spirit-revealed insight into the mind and wisdom of God (1 Cor. 2:10–13). The use of the plural pronouns ('we' and 'us') in this context suggests he saw this as applying not just to himself as an individual, but also to a select group of apostles and prophets responsible for laying the foundation of New Testament doctrine. Paul indicates here that the Spirit's guidance extended beyond thoughts and ideas to words taught by the Spirit. Paul also claims to have apostolic authority (2 Cor. 10:8), divinely authenticated by signs and wonders (2 Cor. 12:12), various visions and revelations from the Lord (2 Cor. 12:1–7), and that he has received his message by revelation directly from Jesus Christ (Gal. 1:11–12; Eph. 3:3–5).

Paul accepts the equal authority of Old and New Testaments. In 1 Timothy 5:18 he supports his case for the financial support of church elders with the following quotations: 'For the Scripture says, "Do not muzzle the ox while it is treading out the grain," and "The worker deserves his wages."' Here he combines a quote from Moses (Deut. 25:4) and another from Jesus (Luke 10:7) in a quotation from 'Scripture', ascribing to both equal Spirit-inspired authority.

Paul claims to have the Spirit of God, the mind of Christ, to speak with the authority of an apostle of Christ. He asserts that Christ is speaking through him (2 Cor. 13:3), and hence his words are endowed with 'the authority of the Lord Jesus' (1 Thess. 4:2). His letters are to be read in the churches and obeyed; the spiritually mature person or true prophet has to recognize his words as a command from the Lord (1 Cor. 14:37). Paul thus expressly claims to speak the word of God: 'when you received the word of God, which you heard from us, you accepted it not as the word of men, but as it actually is, the word of God, which is at work in you who believe' (1 Thess. 2:13).

Peter acknowledges that Paul's writings are to be regarded as part of Scripture:

> He [Paul] writes the same way in all his letters, speaking in them of these matters. His letters contain some things that are hard to understand, which ignorant and unstable people distort, as they do the other Scriptures, to their own destruction. (2 Pet. 3:16)

Peter also claims Scriptural authority for his own writings and those of the other apostles, equating the authority of the Old Testament prophets with that of the New Testament apostles (2 Pet. 3:1–2).

The Paraclete sayings of Jesus give us important insight on the role of the Spirit in revelation. He is characterized as the 'Spirit of truth' (John 14:17), here denoting primarily his opposition to the world, but subsequently his work is described as teaching the disciples and reminding them of his words (John 14:26). The revelatory work of the Holy Spirit thus includes preserving the memory of Jesus and his words for the church. Further light is cast on the Spirit's work of revelation in John 16:12–15. Jesus has 'much more to say' that his disciples will not understand at this point, but describes the future role of the 'Spirit of truth' in this regard. He will guide the Jesus-community into a fuller understanding of Jesus' words and works. What he reveals will, however, be in close continuity with Jesus' teaching: 'He will not speak on his own; he will speak only what he hears . . .' (John 16:13). The Spirit's revealing work thus involves interpreting Jesus to the world, and the ultimate purpose of this revealing ministry is to glorify Jesus (John 16:14–15) (Montague 1976: 349–364).

The church's belief regarding the Spirit's work in connection with Scripture is summarized in the Nicene Creed's brief statement that the Spirit 'spoke by the prophets'. The Spirit of truth thus had a crucial role in the revelation of God's Word to people, and in guiding them to record it in the words of Holy Scripture. In this sense, the Holy Spirit is the author of Scripture, and his inspiration and authorship attests to its divine origin and gives it divine authority.

The Holy Spirit and the human response to Scripture

The Spirit is not only the one who has brought the Word into being, but is also active in the receiving of the Word. The Spirit is not only linked to the work of divine revelation; he is also involved in the human response to that revelation. Several processes were involved between the giving and recording of divine revelation by the original authors and our reception of the Bible as we have it today. *Canonization* is the process by which the inspired books were recognized and included within a certified 'canon' of thirty-nine Old Testament and twenty-seven New Testament books. It is important to clarify that in the process of canonization, the church did not ascribe authority to any of the books of the Bible; rather, it was the recognition of the Spirit's inspiration and apostolic authority of individual books that led to their being recognized as canonical. The Holy Spirit inspired the books, and then guided the canonization process by attesting to its divine authority.

Although there are no extant autographed manuscripts of any of the books of the Bible, over the centuries thousands of manuscript copies have accumulated, through which the text of the Bible has been preserved and transmitted. A critical phase in the transmission of the biblical text, especially since the Protestant Reformation, has been its translation from the original Hebrew, Aramaic and Greek text into the common languages of the world's peoples. Despite the human elements involved in all of these processes, the Spirit's revealing ministry ensures sovereign guidance of all of these stages in the communication of God's revelation to people.

The truth of God's Word needs to be applied to the life of the church and the individual believer. But it is impossible to understand a book authored by the Holy Spirit unless the Spirit himself illuminates our understanding. Here again we see the Spirit of truth exercising his ministry as revealer, teacher and interpreter of the Word. This aspect of the Spirit's revealing ministry is commonly referred to as *illumination*. The need for the Spirit's illumination arises due to two reasons. First, a transcendent and infinite God is beyond the reach of finite humanity's comprehension. It is impossible for human beings to have any meaningful knowledge of God without the help of the Spirit of truth. Secondly, as a result of sin, the whole person – the thinking, feeling and willing self – has become totally unresponsive to the revealed truth of God. Sinful human beings are thus unable to discover the truth of God through unaided reason, experience or some other natural human faculty (Matt. 13:13–15; Mark 8:18; Rom. 1:21; 2 Cor. 4:4). Only through the supernatural guidance of the Spirit of truth can our sin-marred minds grasp God's truth, and apart from the Spirit we would have no understanding of God and his ways. The Spirit opens our ears and hearts to hear God speak through his Word.

Paul speaks of the Holy Spirit revealing and teaching that which we could not otherwise know or understand (1 Cor. 2:14–16; 2 Cor. 4:6). He prays for the Father to bestow 'the Spirit of wisdom and revelation' so the eyes of the heart may be enlightened (Eph. 1:17–18). He speaks of the removal of the veil placed upon the mind so that we may behold the Lord's glory (2 Cor. 3:16–18). John reminds us that the anointing (of the Holy Spirit) enables us to discern the truth and be a reliable teacher and guide to truth (1 John 2:20–21, 27). The New Testament describes this illumination in a variety of ways: listening to the voice of Jesus (John 10:3), having the mind of Christ (1 Cor. 2:16), being filled with all spiritual wisdom and understanding (Col. 1:9), and receiving the gift of understanding to know Jesus (1 John 5:20).

The Holy Spirit exercises his life-giving ministry using truth as the instrument. The necessary condition of spiritual life is revealed truth, but this truth can be received only by the enablement of the Holy Spirit (Lewis and Demarest 1996: 123). The Holy Spirit who inspired the Bible also makes it alive to us as we read it. But the illumination of the Holy Spirit does not guarantee instant and perfect understanding of everything in the Bible. Nor does the 'spiritual' meaning of the text to which the Spirit's illumination leads us entail fanciful interpretations or applications that do not derive naturally from the normal literal meaning of the text (Packer 2005: 240). The Spirit's activity of illumination thus does not furnish new revelation to be added to the canon of Scripture, nor does it make any believer infallible in his interpretation of the biblical text.

It is possible to justify almost anything from the Bible in the name of a Spirit-directed interpretation. A responsible approach to interpreting the Bible involves serious exegetical work, where we try to relate the 'two horizons' of the original text and our present context. We must understand what the writers meant in their own time, before we can interpret that meaning for our time and apply it to our situation. Interpretation is thus a Spirit-led human activity involving exegesis, analysis, synthesis and application of the text, through which we hear God's word for us today.

The illumination of the Spirit does not preclude the effort and hard work required in such study of the Scriptures, but rather presupposes it. The Holy Spirit is thus not just the original author of Scripture, but a living guide and overseer who superintends the interpretation and application of God's Word to the life of the believer. We would benefit much more from our study of the Scriptures if we approached our task with the prayer of Charles Wesley on our lips:

> Come, Holy Ghost, for moved by thee,
> the prophets wrote and spoke;
> unlock the truth, thyself the key,
> unseal the sacred book.
> (From his hymn 'Come, Holy Ghost, our Hearts Inspire')

We thus conclude that the written Scripture together with the inner illumination of the Holy Spirit constitutes authority for the Christian.

There are two extremes to avoid in this regard. There are those whose high view of the Bible as revelation sometimes causes them to view it as having power in itself apart from the Spirit's illumination. This can result in a virtually sacramental view of the Bible, by which it becomes almost a fetish or magical book. This is a tendency in some expressions of fundamental evangelicalism, but we observe it especially in cultures influenced by Islam, Sikhism and Hinduism, where the letter of the Scripture is frequently regarded as having a power of its own. From his early childhood a devout Muslim must learn to recite the Qur'an in Arabic without necessarily understanding a word of what he memorizes. We observe a similar attitude to the Hindu scriptures. For instance, these are read with scrupulous care during a religious ceremony, for the words themselves invoke magical power, and any error in reading could invoke the deity's wrath.

The same impulse leads to the Sikh scriptures, the *Guru Granth Sahib*, being practically worshipped. This was graphically illustrated in the wake of the devastation left by hurricane Katrina in New Orleans, in a newspaper article that recorded the heroic efforts of US-based Sikhs in retrieving a copy of the *Guru Granth Sahib* from a submerged Sikh temple. The degree of value ascribed to the *Granth* itself was seen in the scale and sophistication of the rescue mission. One of the rescuers shared his amazement when, on entering the building, he found the holy book 'floating on five feet of water and untouched by the flood waters', thus tacitly suggesting its magical quality (Rajghatta 2005).

The pre-Christian attitude to their religious scriptures of those who come to faith in Christ from Muslim, Hindu or Sikh backgrounds thus naturally tends to condition their approach to the Bible. The Bible is in itself a reservoir and conduit of God's special revelation, but its words do not have any magical or sacramental power in themselves. The tools of language and interpretation must be employed as we seek to understand the meaning of Scripture. But the Bible will not yield its precious treasures to pure rational and historical investigation. The Holy Spirit, the author of Scripture, must illumine the truth of Scripture and disclose to us its testimony concerning the will and purposes of God.

At the other extreme are those whom the Spirit's illumination leads to a 'spiritual' interpretation that has no relation to the clear meaning of the text. We observe this phenomenon among religious enthusiasts throughout the history of the church, beginning with the second-century Montanists. In our times we find this tendency in various charismatic sects and some quarters of the Pentecostal movement, where the 'word' spoken directly to the believer's spirit is ultimately ascribed greater authority and value than the clear sense of the written text of Scripture.

I recall some years ago hearing a guest speaker from overseas who claimed to have special 'deep' spiritual insight into what John meant in 1 John 3:2: 'Dear friends, now we are children of God, and what we will be has not yet been made known. But we know that when he appears, *we shall be like him*, for we shall see him as he is' (my italics). With deep conviction, this 'inspired' speaker set forth his 'revelation' of the true meaning of this text as follows: God's intention in redemption is not just to fashion us into the image of Christ morally and ethically, but his ultimate vision for the universe is to deify all redeemed people and incorporate them into the being of God! So what Adam and Eve coveted illegally in the Garden of Eden when they yielded to the Serpent's temptation finally becomes part of humankind's experience of 'full' salvation as offered to us in Christ. This bizarre interpretation made me feel distinctly uncomfortable even as a young believer, but the appeal of this 'spiritual' interpretation, based on the authority of superior revelational knowledge, was convincing to many, arousing several 'Amens' of affirmation within the small congregation. One encounters similar strategies of textual interpretation, if perhaps with less serious theological consequences, in popular Pentecostal and charismatic preaching.

The logical conclusion of this tendency to separate the Spirit's witness from that of the Word is spiritualism, where Christ and biblical doctrines become mere symbols of inward mystical realities with little or no continuity with the historic Christian faith. We must insist, on the contrary, that the Holy Spirit does not bring us new revelation, but *new light on God's final revelation* given in Jesus Christ and recorded in holy Scripture.

The Holy Spirit and the Word of God belong together. Just as the Word must always test the spirits, the Holy Spirit must always attest the Word. The Bible does not become the Word of God when people receive it. It is the Word of God whether or not people receive it as such. The Spirit illumines our hearts, enabling us to receive and understand the Bible, the written Word of God. The Bible in turn points us to Jesus Christ, the living Word, the goal and content of divine revelation. Bloesch recommends the following balanced approach:

> In biblical hermeneutics we begin with the natural sense of the passage but . . . proceed to the spiritual sense – the relation of the text to the self revelation of God in Jesus Christ, a relation that is unfolded only by the Spirit working with our spirits to lead us into the knowledge of the truth of the gospel. (Bloesch 2000: 279)

Every student of the Scripture must therefore be open and sensitive to the action of the Spirit. The Spirit through the Word enables believers to walk faithfully with the Lord. Spiritual disciplines such as reading, studying, memorizing and meditating on the Word of God help us to appropriate its message. The continuing illumination of the Holy Spirit through the inner witness of the Holy Spirit is essential to spiritual growth. Faithfulness to Scripture is no substitute for keeping in step with the Spirit; neither is living in the Spirit adequate without obedience to scriptural truth (Lewis and Demarest 1996: 118).

The mutuality of the Spirit and the Word is illustrated vividly in the following simple metaphor. In many parts of the world, matchmakers are highly respected members of the community. Anxious parents of young brides-in-waiting depend on their valued services to be assured of a bright future for their daughters. The matchmaker's arrival is an important event: she must be well treated and fed, honoured, and eventually suitably compensated. But the matchmaker is valued not for who she is in herself but for the role she plays. She comes as a mediator, and her job is to introduce a handsome, well-placed and eligible bridegroom. She comes equipped with suitable tools (bio-data, references and, most importantly, the photographs) all this to one end: selling the bridegroom by highlighting his virtues and exalting his merits. What a beautiful, if imperfect, picture of the ministry of the Spirit of truth!

The Holy Spirit has come to point us to Jesus, the goal and content of divine revelation. He sheds his light on and uses the written Word – his equipment, so to speak – but the ultimate focus of his ministry is to glorify Jesus. His role is first as interpreter, to make clear the truth about him, and then as illuminator, to enable spiritually insensitive hearts to receive this truth. Packer characterizes this graphically as the 'floodlight' ministry of the Spirit, where the purpose of the floodlight is not to draw attention to himself, as much as to make visible and clarify the details of the object on which it is focused. The Spirit is thus 'the hidden floodlight shining on the Saviour' (Packer 2005: 57). The Spirit's self-effacing ministry thus directs all attention away from himself to Christ – faith in Christ, love of Christ, obedience to Christ, worship of Christ and the glory of Christ.

7

Life in the Spirit

The Spirit and Salvation in Christ

The New Testament uses a wide variety of expressions to characterize the work of the Spirit. These include 'clothed with power' (Luke 24:49), 'baptize' (Luke 3:16), 'receive power' (Acts 1:8), 'filled with' (Acts 2:4; 13:9; Eph. 5:18), 'pour out' (Acts 2:17), 'gift' (Acts 2:38), 'controlled' (Rom. 8:9), 'drink' (1 Cor. 12:13) and 'live by' (Gal. 5:16). The richness of terminology describing the Spirit's work reflects, on one hand, the limitations of human language in speaking of the Spirit, and, on the other, the wide range of the Spirit's activity.

Underlying all these expressions, however, is the basic conviction that the Holy Spirit is God personally at work in the lives of the community of God's people. In Jesus' well-known conversation with Nicodemus in John 3, he likens the work of the Spirit to that of the wind: 'The wind blows wherever it pleases. You hear its sound, but you cannot tell where it comes from or where it is going. So it is with everyone born of the Spirit' (John 3:8). The Spirit cannot be seen, but his activity can be observed by its effects and results. No one can claim to belong to Jesus Christ without having his Spirit at work in her (Rom. 8:9). The Christian life is thus lived in the conscious awareness of the presence and power of the Spirit. But like the wind, he is known not in himself but by what he does.

What does the Holy Spirit do? This is the question that will concern us in the remaining chapters of this study. We must, however, recognize at the very outset that the Holy Spirit does not seek to draw attention to himself. He comes to glorify Christ and mediate his presence to us. His task thus involves creating and strengthening our awareness of Jesus' active personal presence and transforming power, and thus deepening our allegiance to, love for and worship of Jesus. We began to look at this in relation to the Spirit's revealing and illuminating work in the previous chapter, and go on now to examine other aspects of the Spirit's work. The Spirit's work is directed towards effecting transformation among the community of believers, but his primary focus is Christ. His concern with the needs of believers is thus subsidiary to his magnificent obsession with Christ.

While the Spirit plays a central role in the work of salvation, we need to make two important preliminary clarifications. First, salvation in Christ includes both the initial entrance into the kingdom by faith in Christ, and the ongoing relationship of remaining 'in Christ' or 'life in the Spirit'. Secondly, salvation in the New Testament is never conceived of in strictly individualistic terms. In salvation, an individual enters the kingdom through faith in Christ and the gift of the Spirit, but she is also incorporated into the people of God. Our focus in this chapter is on the work of salvation as it begins in the heart of the individual; we shall consider the corporate dimension in the following chapter.

The work of the Holy Spirit begins with the 'hearing' of the gospel (Rom. 10:14–15). This involves the revealing and recording of the gospel as God's very word, which must be believed (1 Thess. 2:13; 2 Thess. 2:13). It also includes the work of the Spirit in the act of proclamation and drawing people to Christ. We have already looked at the first of these in the previous chapter; we now turn to the second.

The Spirit and conviction

One of the earliest references to the Spirit in Paul's writings refers to the gospel having come to the Thessalonians 'not simply with words, but also with power, with the Holy Spirit and with deep conviction' (1 Thess. 1:5). Again, in 1 Corinthians 2:1–5, Paul argues that although his preaching lacked persuasive wisdom and rhetoric, it was accompanied by a demonstration of the Spirit's power. In Romans 15:18–19, he insists his preaching all the way from Jerusalem to Illyricum (modern-day Albania and Croatia) was an effective combination of the word and miraculous signs, both of which were 'through the power of the Spirit'. Paul's proclamation of the word was thus in 'power', which includes accompanying signs and wonders and deep conviction by the power of the Spirit. Thus, for Paul, the Spirit's work in salvation begins with Spirit-empowered proclamation that brings conviction of sin and of the truth of the gospel (1 Cor. 14:24–25).

Those without Christ are unable to see, know or receive spiritual things (John 14:17; 1 Cor. 2:14). The Spirit's work in the heart of the unbeliever causes him to turn to the Lord. In John 16:8–11, Jesus speaks of the Holy Spirit's work of conviction: he creates both an awareness of sin and our need for a saviour. He opens blind eyes so that unbelievers may see the truth and respond positively to it. When a person hears the gospel, the Spirit works in her heart, convincing her of the reality of Christ, and draws her to him. This is what Jesus referred to when he said that the Spirit of truth he would send from the Father would 'testify' about him (John 15:26; cf. Acts 5:32).

I recall witnessing this first hand some years ago at a prayer meeting in my home. A friend who was a relatively new Christian had brought along a first-time visitor, a young lady who seemed to be attending a meeting of this nature for the first time, and was clearly feeling out of place. In my mind, I wondered at my friend's wisdom in bringing a first-time visitor to a prayer meeting, concerned that she might find the activity too intense or even boring. I thought the proper occasion to bring a first-time visitor was a more seeker-friendly evangelistic meeting. Imagine my astonishment when, about halfway through the prayer meeting, during a time of spontaneous intercession, I heard an unfamiliar voice break out in prayer. I realized it must have been this young lady, but could hardly believe my ears and opened my eyes for a brief moment just to make sure. She obviously knew something of the gospel but, to the amazement and joy of every believer present, was now spontaneously and openly confessing her sins and surrendering her life to Jesus. The young lady subsequently became a committed member of our prayer group and, years later, remains an active church member.

1 Corinthians 14:24–25 provides us with a striking illustration of how the convicting power of the Holy Spirit works in the context of corporate worship. Although the minds of unbelievers have been blinded by 'the god of this age', Satan (2 Cor. 4:4), the prophetic utterance unveils the darkened mind, penetrates the unbeliever's heart, and lays it bare before all. The conviction of sin thus leads to an enlightened understanding and acceptance of God's revelation in Christ. This faith in Christ is thus both a prior work of the Spirit in the life of a person being drawn to Christ, and a prerequisite for reception of the gift of the Spirit (2 Cor. 4:13; Gal. 3:2–5). The convicting work of the Holy Spirit thus denotes the hearing and understanding of the gospel that leads to faith in Christ.

The Spirit and conversion We have already observed that in the New Testament, salvation in Christ is indispensably linked to reception of the Holy Spirit. From the time of John the Baptist's announcement (Matt. 3:11), the Spirit's bestowal is clearly linked to the ministry of Jesus. While John's Gospel specifically links the giving of the Spirit with the glorification of Jesus (7:37), Peter's Pentecostal sermon states explicitly that the Holy Spirit was poured out as a result of the death, resurrection and subsequent exaltation of Jesus (Acts 2:22–33). The Spirit's work thus involves essentially applying the benefits of Christ's saving work to the human race. Salvation has thus been accomplished by Christ through his death and resurrection, but is effected by the the Holy Spirit, the empowering presence of God.

A crucial text is Galatians 3:2–5, where Paul, in trying to counter the influence of the legalistic 'Judaizers', asks the Galatian believers, 'Did you receive the Spirit by observing the law, or by believing what you heard?' (Gal. 3:2). In challenging the Galatian believers to stand firm in faith, Paul grounds his appeal in their experience of the Spirit. Again, in Titus 3:4–7, Paul emphasizes the crucial role of the Spirit in conversion. The mercy of God our Saviour, not good works, is the basis of our salvation. But this salvation is effected through the regenerating work of the Holy Spirit (Titus 3:5). The New Testament also regularly refers to the conversion experience of believers in terms of the Spirit. Thus God gives, anoints with, pours out and seals with his Spirit (Rom. 5:5; 2 Cor. 1:21; Titus 3:6; Eph. 1:13; 4:30). Likewise, believers have received, been washed, sanctified and justified, and saved through the sanctifying work of the Spirit (1 Cor. 2:12; 6:11; 2 Cor. 11:4; Rom. 15:16; 2 Thess. 2:13). The role of the Spirit in the work of conversion is thus highlighted unmistakably in the New Testament.

But what is the nature of the Spirit's work in conversion? Is it to be thought of essentially in terms of a new birth or a baptism by the Spirit? Are these to be thought of as one and the same experience of 'initiation' into the kingdom? Or should they be distinguished into two stages: new birth by the Spirit (intiation) and baptism in the Spirit (vocational)? What about adoption, sanctification and anointing by the Spirit? Conflicting theological viewpoints on some of these great themes have been the source of much discussion and debate among Bible-believing Christians for centuries.

I shall not attempt to resolve the debate on any of these questions in this brief study, nor do I intend to generate fresh controversy by my treatment of these themes. There is, in fact, much more agreement among these seemingly differing viewpoints than we often realize, and it is my purpose to draw attention to the areas where there is broad consensus of evangelical opinion, without glossing over the real differences that exist. A critical first step in trying to chart a course through the maze of theological opinion is to recognize that the New Testament uses a variety of metaphors in describing the Spirit's role in the work of salvation. Just as metaphors such as redemption, justification, reconciliation and propitiation are used in relation to Christ's saving work, so metaphors are used that emphasize the distinctive role of the Spirit in salvation, including life-giving, rebirth, washing, adoption, sanctification, baptism, earnest, seal, first fruits and anointing.

We shall look more closely at the more prominent of these metaphors in trying to understand the Spirit's role in the conversion experience. It is, however, important to note that the use of a wide variety of images indicates that the work of the Spirit, as of Christ, is too complex to be captured by any one metaphor. The metaphors are selected and used in keeping with the need of the context, and the aspect of the human condition being addressed. Thus, for instance, the metaphor of 'life-giving' is used with respect to the predicament of humankind being 'dead in . . . transgressions and sins' (Eph. 2:1); 'washing' (Titus 3:5) as an antidote to the uncleanness of sin; 'rebirth' (1 Pet. 1:23) in response to the human need for a radical new beginning. The critical underlying constant in all these metaphors that must be emphasized is that, however expressed, the vital agency and active presence of the Holy Spirit is essential to the Christian experience of conversion.

The Spirit as life-giver

The Bible teaches that the root cause of the human problem is sin in the human race. Sin is a deep and deadly spiritual disease that has corrupted the human heart and infected the entire human race (Mark 7:20–23; Rom. 3:23; 7:7–9). The most serious consequence of sin is death in the deepest sense of the word (spiritual death, separation from God), of which physical death is only a sign and tangible reminder (Gen. 2:17; Rom. 6:23). The Bible thus describes man apart from Christ as 'dead in . . . transgressions and sins' (Eph. 2:1). The only real antidote to death is life, and that is what salvation in Christ is all about – giving new life to those spiritually dead because of their alienation or separation from God.

Christ as the source of life is a recurring theme in John's Gospel. His life was 'the light of men' (1:4); he came 'that they may have life, and have it to the full' (10:10); he is 'the bread of life' (6:35), also 'the resurrection and the life'

(11:25); through him all people can have 'eternal life' (3:36; 4:14; 5:24). Christ thus came to bring new life, eternal life, life in all its fullness, to all humankind, but it is the Holy Spirit who plays a crucial role in actually imparting this new life to those who will receive it.

For Paul, the Spirit is the 'Spirit of life' who 'gives life' to those who turn to Christ (Rom. 8:2, 6; 2 Cor. 3:6). The unbeliever who is 'dead in . . . transgressions and sins' is brought to life by the coming of the life-giving Spirit. Conversion thus involves a radical reorientation of one's entire life. Just as Christ died and rose again, the believer likewise experiences death and resurrection through the power of the life-giving Spirit (Rom. 6:1–6; Col. 2:20–3:4). Becoming a believer in Christ thus means being given new life by the Spirit himself, resulting in a new creation (2 Cor. 5:17).

I heard a testimony in chapel last week that illustrates this powerfully and dramatically. Ranjit, a final-year theology student, had everyone spellbound as he narrated his story. In a sordid tale of delinquency and crime he recounted his experiences as a drug trafficker and gangster. Ranjit finally found himself on a hospital bed desperately ill. A vital blood vessel close to his lungs had been punctured, causing him to cough up blood from his lungs every fifteen minutes. The nearest city where the needed surgery could be performed was several hours away and he would never survive the journey. Ranjit's friends joined him as they wept, resigning themselves to the inevitable. As Ranjit lay awake in the night, in the dim light of the hospital room he noticed on the wall to the right of his bed a faded picture of a figure on a cross. He remembered vaguely the story of Jesus raising someone from the dead after three days. Clutching desperately at this slender thread of hope, he prayed, 'Jesus, if you could raise that man from the dead, surely you can raise me from this bed . . . if you give me my life, I will give it back to you.'

The next morning Ranjit was visited by a stranger who offered to pray with him. At first he was suspicious, but then, to his amazement, the stranger turned his Bible to the account of Jesus raising Lazarus from the dead, which he read before he prayed. According to Ranjit, by evening the bleeding had mysteriously stopped, confounding even the doctor treating him. Ranjit walked out of the hospital two days later, weak but well, having received a new lease of physical life and new spiritual life in Christ, both through the life-giving Spirit.

Washing/rebirth by the Spirit

The Spirit's life-giving function is closely associated with two terms that occur frequently together: washing and rebirth / new birth or regeneration. The classic text is Jesus' famous words to Nicodemus: 'No-one can see the kingdom of God unless he is born again . . . no-one can enter the kingdom of God unless he is born of water and the Spirit' (John 3:3, 5). The word translated 'again' is probably better translated 'from above', consistent with its rendering subsequently in the same context, where it refers to 'the one who comes *from above* . . .' (John 3:31). It was thus simply an indirect way of stating that a person must experience a birth from God in order to enter the kingdom of God.

Jesus' mention of 'water' in this instance has been thought variously to refer to physical birth, water baptism or, metaphorically, either to the Word of God or the Spirit of God. Turner argues that the special construction 'of water-and-Spirit' 'must refer to a unitary event, a single metaphorical "birth" accomplished through some sort of combination of water and Spirit' (Turner 1998: 68; cf. Bloesch 2000: 303–304). This eliminates the possible suggestion of natural birth, and reference to Christian baptism is unlikely, since Jesus assumes that Nicodemus should be able to understand what he is saying. The most natural and likely interpretation reads 'and' as meaning 'that is', so that 'and the Spirit' is understood as simply an explanation of the phrase 'born of water'.

Water was an accepted symbol of the Holy Spirit, used by Jesus himself elsewhere in John's Gospel (John 7:37–39). If, as scholars have observed, the background of this discourse derives from God's promise in Ezekiel 'I will sprinkle clean water on you . . . I will give you a new heart and put a new spirit in you . . . And I will put my Spirit in you . . .' (Ezek. 36:25–27), this would make sense to Nicodemus, even if the idea of regeneration was unfamiliar to him (Turner 1998: 68–69; Williams 1980: 136–137). Thus, although an indirect allusion to baptism may be present, being 'born of water' does not refer to anything external that is complementary to the inward work of the Spirit, but to the inner cleansing renewal the Spirit effects.

The metaphor as employed here highlights the fact that conversion involves a radical new beginning where God himself regenerates a person through the agency of the Holy Spirit. Although human choice and response are clearly involved in conversion, Jesus' explanation in this context seems to emphasize the sovereignty of the Spirit's activity in this regard. Just as we had nothing to do with our natural birth, so we can do nothing about our own spiritual rebirth: it is altogether a work of God.

The metaphors of 'washing' and 'rebirth/renewal' are used together in Titus 3:5, where Paul declares, 'He [God] saved us through the washing of rebirth and renewal by the Holy Spirit'. This is a difficult sentence to interpret, and some see it as distinguishing between two experiences, possibly referring to baptism ('washing of rebirth') and confirmation ('renewal by the Holy Spirit') within the sacramental traditions, or, correspondingly, by Pentecostals as conversion-baptism and the baptism in the Holy Spirit. Others, however, see it as referring to one experience of 'washing' that involves rebirth and renewal. Although the allusion to baptism is undeniable, the emphasis is clearly on the salvific role of the Spirit in effecting rebirth and renewal. The 'washing' metaphor also appears in 1 Corinthians 6:11, where again, despite a possible allusion to baptism, the emphasis clearly is on the Spirit's agency in cleansing sin.

The Spirit thus not only cleanses people from past sins but also transforms them through rebirth and renewal so they begin to reflect God's nature in their lives.

The Spirit of adoption

In Galatians 4:4–6, Paul contrasts living under the law with life in the Spirit. The evidence that we are children of God is our experience of the Spirit, by whom we call God 'Abba, Father'. According to Fee, the Aramaic term Abba that Jesus uses to address the Father, expresses the language of children of all ages, denoting both intimacy and special relatedness (Fee 1994: 857). At first glance it sounds as though Paul regards sonship as prior to reception of the Spirit. Paul is, however, simply describing how the believer's experience of 'sonship' by the Spirit is contingent on the objective reality of 'sonship' Christ provides by his death on the cross. The parallel passage in Romans 8:15–17 thus states clearly that by their reception of the Spirit believers become the adopted children of God and are able to cry 'Abba, Father'. The certain proof of our entrance into God's family is that we speak to God in the language of family. It indicates that we have entered into all the privileges and responsibilities of a person who has been adopted as a child in God's family.

Spirit-baptism and spiritual gifts

The metaphor of baptism as used in relation to the Spirit has been the focus of much attention in the recent past and hence warrants separate treatment. The New Testament has seven references to the metaphor of baptism in relation to the activity of the Spirit. Of these, six contrast the baptism of John the Baptist with that of Jesus. Whereas John baptized with water for repentance, Jesus would baptize with the Holy Spirit. The references in the four Gospels all occur as part of the Baptist's testimony in the context of his baptizing Jesus (Matt. 3:11; Mark 1:8; Luke 3:16; John 1:33). The first reference in Acts records the words of Jesus: 'Do not leave Jerusalem, but wait for the gift my Father promised, which you have heard me speak about. For John baptized with water, but in a few days you will be baptized with the Holy Spirit' (Acts 1:4–5). In the second instance, Peter recalls these words of Jesus in explaining the outpouring of the Holy Spirit upon Cornelius' household (Acts 11:16). The only other reference is in 1 Corinthians 12:13: 'For we were all baptized by one Spirit into one body – whether Jews or Greeks, slave or free – and we were all given the one Spirit to drink.'

The term 'baptism' implies to be immersed in, plunged under, and even drenched or soaked, suggesting that the whole being of a person is imbued with or enveloped in the Holy Spirit. But two crucial questions arise in relation to the Spirit's role in baptism: (1) *What is the relationship, if any, between the Spirit's work and water baptism?* (2) *Does the Bible teach an experience subsequent to conversion called the 'baptism in the Holy Spirit'?* The first is a matter especially close to the heart of those from Christian sacramental traditions; the second, a concern that emerges from within the Pentecostalcharismatic movement.

In Bloesch's observation, 'One of the perennial controversies in the history of the church has been the mysterious relation of water and Spirit baptism' (Bloesch 2000: 279). In the New Testament, water baptism is commonly an outward sign of conversion and faith in Christ, the immediate response of the new believer to the saving action of the Spirit. Many have thus seen water baptism as effectively mediating the saving action of the Spirit. Kilian McDonnell, a Roman Catholic charismatic scholar says, 'By the sacrament of baptism one becomes a member of the body of Christ because in baptism one receives the Spirit' (quoted in Williams 1990: 283). See also Jensen's Lutheran statement 'The giving of the Spirit stands in the closest possible relationship to baptism with water. To be baptized with Christian baptism (water and the Word) is to receive the gift of the Holy Spirit' (quoted in Bloesch 2000: 279). Again, F. D. Bruner writes, 'Baptism and the reception of the Spirit are so synonymous as to be identical. Christian baptism is spiritual baptism' (quoted in Williams 1990: 283).

In contrast, Rodman Williams insists there is no biblical basis for maintaining any essential connection between water baptism and Spirit baptism:

> None of the narratives in Acts represent the Holy Spirit as being given through water baptism . . . there is no suggestion that such baptism is the medium or channel. Even less is water baptism portrayed as conferring the gift of the Spirit. The Holy Spirit comes from the exalted Lord who . . . surely does not relegate such to a rite conducted by man. (Williams 1990: 282)

After assessing all the textual evidence in Paul's writings, the New Testament scholar Gordon Fee convincingly argues that 'in no text does Paul associate the gift of the Spirit with water baptism, either as cause and effect or as occurring experientially at the same time', and insists that Paul instead consistently regarded the reception of the Spirit to take place at conversion, with the proclamation of the gospel and its reception by faith (Fee 1994: 862). Another New Testament scholar, James Dunn, makes a similar observation regarding the Fourth Gospel, maintaining that John never ties the Spirit's activity to a sacramental rite, nor does he view the Spirit 'as given through Christian baptism, let alone through the water of Christian baptism' (Dunn 1970: 189, 191).

While water is frequently used metaphorically in Scripture as an agent of cleansing and renewal, it is difficult to defend on scriptural grounds the doctrine of baptismal regeneration as held by 'full-blown' sacramentalists. But a view of the sacrament that sees water baptism as not in any way mediating the Holy Spirit, rather pointing beyond itself to the gracious bestowal of the Spirit of God, is commonly affirmed by many evangelicals holding allegiance to sacramental traditions.

In recent times, the phenomenon of Spirit-baptism, or more popularly 'baptism in/with the Holy Spirit', has become a central theme, resulting especially from the influence of the Pentecostal-charismatic movement. In broad terms, it tries to relate the New Testament description of the Spirit's empowerment of the earliest Christians to the experience of believers today. While all Bible-believing Christians affirm the importance of Spirit-baptism and empowerment, there are differences regarding its precise nature and its relationship to conversion.

The Protestant sacramental view simply identifies Spirit-baptism with water baptism. As we have seen in the preceding paragraphs, according to this view, the sacrament of water baptism does not merely symbolize, but actually effects, conversion accompanied by the reception of the Spirit. The common Roman Catholic belief is a two-stage version of this sacramental view, according to which it is not baptism alone, but baptism followed subsequently by confirmation through the laying on of hands by a bishop, by means of which the Holy Spirit is received. The evangelical Protestant view identifies the baptism in the Holy Spirit with conversion: a person is baptized in the Holy Spirit when she repents and submits her life to the lordship of Christ. Pentecostals and some charismatics hold to a two-stage view of the bestowal of the Spirit. They distinguish between a first stage 'initiation' by the Spirit in conversion, resulting in the indwelling by the Spirit, and a second stage 'vocational' empowerment of the Spirit, the experience described as 'the baptism in/with the Holy Spirit'. Many sacramental charismatics have found creative alternatives to this view, explaining Spirit-baptism in terms of a fresh release of grace already present within the believer through the sacraments of baptism and confirmation (Gaybba 1987: 248–249).

The principal lines of debate among evangelical Christians focus on two issues: (1) The question of subsequence, of a two-stage bestowal of the Spirit; (2) the ongoing validity and role of the spectacular or so-called extraordinary gifts, such as tongues, prophecy, healing, exorcism and miracles.

Spirit baptism and 'subsequence'

Much has been written and considerable argument exchanged on the issue of the baptism of the Holy Spirit as an experience distinct from and subsequent to conversion or regeneration by the Spirit. The last few decades have seen the exegetical issues discussed in such great length and detail that it would be presumptuous to try to add anything of exegetical substance to either side of the debate. My desire is not to avoid the real exegetical issues, to side-step theological criticisms of the Pentecostal movement, or to try to defend either the evangelical interpretation or the charismatic response. My intent is rather, in resonance with the spirit of the Lausanne Covenant, to look beyond some of the real differences to significant areas of convergence, often obscured in the heat of the debate.

1. All evangelicals (Reformed, Lutheran, Baptist, Pentecostal and charismatic) affirm the biblical teaching that salvation is by grace through faith in the finished work of Christ on the cross of Calvary, on the basis of which the Holy Spirit is bestowed. All likewise insist that the work of the life-giving Spirit in conversion results in rebirth, the indwelling of the Spirit and adoption into the family of God. Thus, with the exception of a few extreme, sectarian Pentecostals, those on both sides of the divide accept unreservedly their mutual sharing in the fellowship of the Spirit. Evangelicals who differ from the Pentecostal position on Spirit-baptism do not on that basis contradict the genuineness of Pentecostal conversion experiences. Pentecostals, for their part, generally do not deny the validity of the claims of conversion and the Spirit's indwelling by those who do not accept the Pentecostal belief in the baptism in the Holy Spirit. On the essential questions of the basis of membership in the family of God and fellowship in the Holy Spirit, evangelicals on both sides of the debate share the same biblical and theological stance.

Problems arise, on one hand, when the Pentecostal emphasis tends to perpetuate division between those who have 'it' (the Pentecostal experience) and those who do not. Critics of the Pentecostal movement object to the arrogance and elitism implicit in the claim by some Christians to possess more of the Holy Spirit than others. Pentecostals for their part feel their quest for an experience of the Spirit's presence and power is in accordance with the New Testament description and promise, and thus legitimate. They are frequently denigrated by some evangelicals whose reading of the biblical text is conditioned by their own experience.

2. On closer reflection, the question of 'subsequence' and even the essential content of the Pentecostal experience appear to be less of an issue than they are often made out to be. The Roman Catholic practice of confirmation reflects an early Christian tradition that recognized the need for a fuller bestowal of the Spirit subsequent to baptism. This is corroborated amply by many exponents within both Catholic and Protestant mystical traditions. As we have seen, some seventeenth-century Puritans spoke of an experience similar to Pentecostal Spirit-baptism, which they called 'the sealing of the Spirit'. John Wesley and his followers in the eighteenth and nineteenth centuries spoke of a 'second work of grace' subsequent to conversion. A number of significant nineteenth and early twentieth-century figures owned by the evangelical movement as a whole, including Charles Finney, D. L. Moody, A. B. Simpson, R. A. Torrey, Andrew Murray and Watchman Nee, espoused

some form of deeper experience of the Spirit, distinct from conversion, which greatly enhanced the quality of their Christian life and witness.

In fact, most evangelicals would probably not dispute the legitimacy of a special enablement or 'filling' by the Spirit (Matt. 4:1; Acts 13:9) in the context of specific needs or circumstances. Turner resorts to this explanation of the Pentecostal post-conversion experience in concluding his sophisticated refutation of the Pentecostal view of Spirit-baptism. He interprets all Pentecostal-charismatic experience 'as renewing, ongoing and extending experiences or appropriations of the one gift of the Spirit given to all Christians in conversion-initiation' (Turner 1998: 164). Ironically, Lederle's criticism of sacramental explanations of the charismatic experience that Turner cites approvingly could legitimately be levelled towards Turner's own view:

> There is a sense of unreality in telling someone who has just had a powerful renewal experience that theologically nothing has happened at that particular time or that the Holy Spirit did not come in any new way at all, and that all that transpired was that the Spirit, received at baptism [in Turner's view, 'at conversion-initiation'], was experientially 'released' . . . (Turner 1998: 163)

Thus, while most Pentecostals may not find Turner's explanation of their experience convincing, he doubtless expresses a widespread evangelical belief that our encounter with the Spirit can never be a one-time experience that lasts for the rest of our lives. We sin, grieve and quench the Spirit; we become weary and spiritually dry; we face situations simply beyond our ability to handle. All evangelicals will acknowledge that such situations call for a fresh touch of the Holy Spirit. The Spirit who has come must, in a sense, keep on coming, leading us into new realms of his grace and power. This is what Paul meant when he exhorted the Ephesians to *keep on being filled* with the Spirit (Eph. 5:18).

The points of contention include the decisive emphasis Pentecostals place on one such experience of special enablement by the Spirit, the focus on the accompanying manifestation (normally glossolalia) and, of course, nomenclature – the characterization of this experience as a Spirit-baptism. The significance of these issues must not be minimized, especially since they do have real practical pastoral implications on both sides. Pentecostals feel that their emphasis stirs people from spiritual complacency and motivates deeper consecration, although critics would say it frequently creates distress and despair among those whose quest for such a deeper experience remains frustrated. Those holding to the 'one-stage' conversion-initiation view of Spirit-baptism, feel their belief places the rightful emphasis on God's sovereignty and faith rather than human effort, but face the charismatic criticism of practising a passive faith, cheapening grace and lacking in spiritual zeal.

Although it may be a source of disappointment to some readers, I shall not attempt to evaluate or pass a verdict on this issue. My purpose is neither to intensify the controversy nor to deepen the divide, but rather to weigh established differences in the context of the deeper continuity of faith and experience of the Spirit shared by all evangelicals, whether or not they embrace the distinctive Pentecostal viewpoint.

The fact is that no significant theological affirmation concerning the Holy Spirit is in question here: the deity and full personhood of the Holy Spirit, his identity as a co-equal member of the Trinity, his inspiration and illumination of the Bible, his life-giving and regenerating work, his indwelling presence in believers, the necessity of his sanctifying and empowering ministry for the life and mission of the church. There is considerable unanimity about all of these issues. Packer points out that this commonality extends to much of the devotional practice of evangelicals and charismatics, who

> are plainly at one in relation to such supposedly evangelical distinctives as faith and repentance; love to the Lord Jesus Christ, who forgives and saves; lives changed by the Spirit's power; learning about God from God through Scripture; bold, expectant, intimate free-form prayer; small group ministry; and a delight in swinging singing. (Packer 2005: 141)

It thus appears as if attitude rather than any substantial theological conviction is the real issue here. Pentecostals frequently express their convictions with an air of spiritual superiority and elitism, while their evangelical counterparts are sometimes equally arrogant in the contempt with which they dismiss Pentecostal teaching and practice as shallow and biblically unsound. If Pentecostals could shed some of their spiritual arrogance and their dialogue partners approach them with a little more respect and openness, there is much room for mutual enrichment, without either side feeling the need to make any significant theological compromise. The bottom line is that both sides accept the centrality of the Spirit's personal, life-giving activity in conversion and Christian growth as affirmed in Scripture.

The gifts of the Spirit

When we turn to the question of the ongoing validity and role of the so-called extraordinary gifts, we observe again that except for the fanatical and fundamental fringes of the evangelical and Pentecostal movements, the issues are rarely of serious theological consequence. The real challenges to biblical Christianity would appear to come from two extreme positions: fundamentalist 'cessationism' on one side and what Packer calls charismatic 'eudaemonism' on the other (Packer 2005: 157).

Charismatic 'eudaemonism' describes the shallow triumphalism prevalent among some sections of the Pentecostal-charismatic movement based upon an 'over-realized' eschatology. According to this prescription of the Spirit-filled life, a believer should always be perfectly healthy, rich and happy. Sickness, want or adversity of any kind is an indication of spiritual illness, the result of sin, demonic activity, divine displeasure or a curse. This approach to the Christian life has to ignore massive scriptural evidence to the contrary of unhealed sickness among believers; of sincere Christians being in financial need and warnings against the 'deceitfulness' of riches; and the inevitability of trials and tribulations for the believer on the road to Christian maturity. Worse still are the pastoral consequences of this caricature of the Spirit-filled life.

One of several instances I recall is especially bizarre, involving a Pentecostal pastor in the last stages of terminal cancer. Another pastor, who subscribed to the 'health and wealth' gospel, paid him a visit, but within moments of receiving prayer for healing the sick man breathed his last and died. Totally unfazed, the visiting pastor turned to the grief-stricken wife and, shaking his head, said, 'If your husband and you had more faith, he would not have died.' The gross insensitivity is unbelievable, but a teaching inconsistent with Scripture can never be true to life as well. A distorted understanding of spiritual well-being that equates it with materialistic wealth creates a grossly misleading hierarchy of spirituality. The rich can be deceived into an illusory sense of spiritual superiority despite being spiritually bankrupt, while a sincere believer trapped in a vortex of material poverty, the victim of a sinfully social construct of caste, race or gender prejudice, can experience a false but devastating sense of spiritual alienation.

Fundamentalist 'cessationism' appears a relatively less formidable threat to biblical Christianity, especially since it claims a more respectable vintage beginning with some post-Nicene fathers such as Chrysostom,

Augustine, Gregory the Great, through Aquinas and Calvin to Warfield in the early twentieth century. The 'hard' form in which modern cessationism is frequently articulated is perhaps unparalleled in the history of the church. In the cessationist position, the miracles in the Bible serve a specific function of attesting the revelation of God in Christ. This role of miracles, according to these proponents, ceased with the recording of this revelation in Scripture. They accordingly assert that the New Testament anticipates the cessation of miraculous gifts, and that they in fact disappeared in church history.

Up to this point cessationism is merely a theological viewpoint that can be contested through an academic assessment of the arguments. For instance, Turner offers a closely argued refutation of the cessationist appeal to the New Testament and church history in support of its case (Turner 1998: 290–302). The cessationist position, however, cannot be coherent unless it also affirms that there are no contemporary counterparts to the miraculous gifts of the New Testament. This is problematic at two critical points. First, the Pentecostal-charismatic movement has over the hundred years of its history accumulated a tradition, at the heart of which is a cumulative narrative of testimonies of God's supernatural intervention in the lives of ordinary people. These testimonies are replete with illustrations of what is often to the recipient an indisputably miraculous occurrence, evidence sometimes of God's grace, love and reality, and at other times of Christ's power over false gods or demons.

The logic of the cessationist argument forces its proponents to relegate such testimonies into one of two categories. Since God does not work in this way any more, these experiences must be either spurious or demonic. What would it feel like for a person to learn that the life-transforming experience of healing or deliverance that led to her receiving Jesus as Lord and Saviour was really either inspired by some minion of Satan or based ultimately on an illegitimate claim? The situation is strikingly similar to the dilemma faced by the blind man Jesus healed in John 9. The Pharisees who cross-examined him tried to undermine his healing, since Jesus' action in healing this man on the sabbath did not fit within their theological framework. The man's starting point was rightly the spectacular outcome of his personal encounter with Jesus: 'Whether he is a sinner or not, I don't know. One thing I do know. I was blind but now I see!' (John 9:25).

Rather than revise their theology based on the evidence before them, the Pharisees tried to suppress it. The healed man was understandably incredulous:

Now that is remarkable! You don't know where he comes from, yet
he opened my eyes. We know that God does not listen to sinners. He
listens to the godly man who does his will . . . If this man were not
from God, he could do nothing. (John 9:30–33)

This was too much for the Pharisees to take, who came clean about what they
really thought: ' "You were steeped in sin at birth; how dare you lecture us!"
And they threw him out' (John 9:34). In fact, their theological presuppositions
not only restricted Jesus from healing on the sabbath, but also did not allow
for a man paying the penalty for his sin with congenital blindness to be healed
by God. Such a theological framework is at best pathetically myopic and at
worst blasphemous!

This leads us to the second major difficulty with cessationism: the
arbitrary limits it seems to place on God's sovereignty and providence.
Even a 'soft' cessationist like Packer concedes that 'no sober Catholic or
Protestant when challenged will seriously deny that God can reproduce all
the phenomena of the New Testament at any time, if he so wills' (Packer 2005:
149). The reason for this is obvious. What is really at stake is our view of
God and how we interpret the biblical account of his nature and acts. Is God
actively present in the world and in the church today? Does he convict the
sinner, illuminate his Word, offer guidance? Does he hear and answer the
prayers of his children? If God does intervene in human affairs sovereignly
or in response to prayer, how else can we describe it except in terms of
miraculous intervention?

The world views of the vast majority of people in the nonWestern world
share a fundamental presupposition that the God of the Bible must be living
and engaged in the affairs of his world, or he is no God at all. The cessationist
arguments are simply untrue to the way things are in the experience of many
of these pre-literate, but radiant, believers in Jesus. While sometimes unable
to read the Bible stories they love so dearly, they nonetheless live in the
supernatural world of the Bible through their vital experience of the Spirit.

8

The Community of the Spirit

The Spirit and the Church

We have noted in chapter 2 that the New Testament church was born with the coming of the Holy Spirit upon the earliest disciples of Jesus on the day of Pentecost. In his use of the 'body' analogy to describe the essential nature and identity of the church, Paul clarifies that this 'one body' consists of all who share the same experience of being immersed and having drunk deeply of the Spirit (1 Cor. 12:13). The church thus comprises the people of God who share a common experience of renewal and transformation by the Spirit. The church was created and formed by the Spirit, and may be described properly as a fellowship or community *of the Spirit*.

In this chapter, we shall explore more closely the vital link between the Spirit and the church. We shall first examine what the Bible teaches about the Spirit's role in relation to the church's identity, and then attempt to understand how the Spirit enables the church to fulfil its mission in the world. The nature and functions of the church are organically and inseparably linked. However, despite the overlap at certain points, the logical distinction drawn between the church's identity and mission in this treatment is helpful for our discussion.

The church's identity as the community of the Spirit

We examine here the Spirit's work in making the church the church. What is the church as God intended her to be and what is the Spirit's role in affecting this identity?

The Spirit makes the church the dwelling place of God

In the Old Testament, God's presence among his people was represented by tabernacle and temple. This imagery provides the background for the New Testament descriptions of the Spirit's presence in the midst of God's people. In fulfilment of the Old Testament promise, the living God is now present with his people, based on the new covenant as instituted by Christ. A temple is the place of God's dwelling, and the Holy Spirit is the way God dwells in his holy temple, both in the individual believer and in the church. What makes the church, the gathered community of believers, God's temple, the dwelling place of God, is the presence of the Spirit in their midst (1 Cor. 3:16–17; Eph. 2:19–22).

I live in a part of the world where temples and other places of worship are a common sight. Some of these are historical monuments, magnificent edifices representing works of architectural genius, attracting millions of pilgrims from all over the world down through the centuries. Others are small roadside shrines, frequently consisting of a small slab of stone or a figurine no bigger than a child's toy. What all of these have in common is that they capture for the devotee an awareness of the holy and transcendent. Pilgrims must remove their footwear before they enter; travellers must stop and fold their hands or present an offering to the shrine before they continue their journey. While expressions may differ in detail, the basic sentiment is universal. A temple is a place where God dwells, and the realization of God's presence always evokes reverence and awe among the devout among people of all faiths. People in our world are hungry for a genuine experience with God, and the church, designed by God to be his dwelling place, should be well equipped to meet this need.

In the context of his instructions to the Corinthians concerning the proper exercise of spiritual gifts, Paul suggests that when the church comes together for worship, God's presence must be so evident that the unbeliever who walks in will experience conviction: 'the secrets of his heart will be laid bare. So he will fall down and worship God, exclaiming, "God is really among you!" ' (1 Cor. 14:25). Paul's words should challenge any local body of believers anywhere in the world to so vibrant an experience of God's presence that it would elicit a similar response from people of all faiths or no faith who visit the church.

The Spirit makes the church the body of Christ

This imagery is very prominent in New Testament descriptions of the church, and is used to illustrate two important truths concerning the church. First, Christ's headship of the church is emphasized (Eph. 1:22–23; 4:15; 5:23; Col. 2:10; 2:19), and secondly, the church's unity and diversity, both of which are the work of 'one and the same Spirit' (1 Cor. 12:11–12).

The essential unity of God's people is clearly presupposed by the body analogy. Although composed of both Jew and Gentile, common access by one Spirit to the Father and common participation in this one Spirit makes them one body (Eph. 2:18; 1 Cor. 12:13). The unity the one Spirit has effected among God's people, making them one body, must thus be maintained and disunity resisted (Eph. 4:3–4; 1 Cor. 12:21–26). Healthy diversity is, however, also the result of the Spirit's work (1 Cor. 12:14–20). A body cannot consist of only one part; for the community to be built up, there must be diversity. The Spirit responsible for the unity of the body also provides the many parts and functions necessary for the body's healthy growth and sustenance.

The mandate of Christian unity derives originally from the words of Jesus himself in his prayer recorded in John 17: 'I pray . . . that all of them may be one, Father, just as you are in me and I am in you. May they also be in us so that the world may believe that you have sent me' (John 17:20–21). Unity according to the prayer of Jesus is thus a necessary precondition for effective witness. The unity the Spirit effects breaks down the wall that separates Jews and Gentiles when they come to faith in Christ, breaks down the hostility between people of different races and nationalities, and leaves no room for distinctions based on gender, wealth, caste, class or social status.

Disunity in the body is thus a deadly ailment and a serious negation of the claims of Christ as proclaimed by the church. This is why Paul attacks this tendency so severely in addressing this problem in the first three chapters of his first letter to the Corinthian church. His warning is unmistakable: the person who creates dissension or furthers division in the body is guilty of trying to destroy the church, God's temple, and 'If anyone destroys God's temple, God will destroy him . . .' (1 Cor. 3:17).

The unity of the body of Christ, which the Spirit creates, is thus a spiritual reality that affects the lives of people in practical ways, resulting in concrete expressions of love, reconciliation, forgiveness, acceptance and accountability. When these marks of the Spirit's reality are present as expressions of healthy corporate body life, they help validate the claims of Jesus Christ, and unbelievers are spontaneously attracted to him.

The Spirit makes the church the family of God

The church is 'God's household' (Eph. 2:19; 1 Tim. 3:15), where God himself is Father and believers are brothers and sisters. The Spirit is responsible for and affords evidence of believers' membership in the family of God. In Romans 8:14–17, he is described as 'the Spirit of adoption' who prompts believers to cry, '*Abba*, Father', expressing intimacy and echoing the language of Jesus in addressing the Father. The believer's experience of the Spirit is thus the basis of his identity as a child of God and provides subjective assurance that he belongs to the family of God.

Psychologists tell us that one of the basic needs of every human being is the need to belong. The need for unconditional acceptance is a universal impulse with psychological, emotional, social and spiritual dimensions. God designed the institution of family as an essential means for meeting these needs. While God does intend for the family to meet real needs here on earth, it is, however, in many ways a type and pointer to the ultimate 'perfect' family (Father, Son and Holy Spirit) to which every human being is invited to belong.

This results in the New Testament *koinōnia* (fellowship) of the Holy Spirit, mentioned, for instance, in Paul's benediction in 2 Corinthians 13:14, 'May the grace of the Lord Jesus Christ, and the love of God, and the *fellowship* of the Holy Spirit be with you all' (my italics). We have looked at this beautiful term earlier in chapter 5, and its meaning: having in common or sharing of life. The Spirit thus works as the 'Go-between God', going between Jesus and the church, mediating the life, love and power of Jesus to believers and enabling them to participate in one another's lives as they share in a common life of the Spirit:

> The concept of *koinōnia* . . . begins as fellowship with God through Christ (1 Cor. 1:9), which in turn brings believers into fellowship with one another. . . . Although (in 2 Cor. 13:13–14) this refers chiefly to 'a common participation in the Spirit himself', such participation is common to them all and thus also includes the 'fellowship' created and sustained by the Spirit. (Fee 1994: 872)

As pointed out in the earlier discussion, although the concept is grounded in the inner life of the Trinity, this is not meant to be just a spiritual ideal, but a concrete, lived-out experience of community. The book of Acts describes the expression of this *koinōnia* in the early church as follows:

> All the believers were together and had everything in common. Selling their possessions and goods, they gave to anyone as he had need . . . They broke bread in their homes and ate together with glad and sincere hearts . . . And the Lord added to their number daily those who were being saved. (Acts 2:44–47)

While the specific expressions of *koinōnia* may vary depending on socio-economic and cultural factors, the principle of shared life is clearly to be lived out by communities of believers at all times everywhere.

In the majority-world Christian communities it is usual to find young converts ostracized from their pre-Christian kinship groups and families. These young people pay a great price for following Jesus and would be hopelessly isolated but for Christian families in the church who adopt them as their own, providing them a home away from home. Christians in North America or Europe sometimes also do this with foreign students or with refugee immigrants. The church's record in this is, however, blemished and frequently inconsistent. Converts from Muslim backgrounds especially find the Christian community ethic weak in contrast to the strong feeling of brotherhood found in most Islamic communities.

I once heard the Croatian evangelical leader Dr Peter Kuzmic share this powerful testimony of Christian community from pre-perestroika days in Eastern Europe. In illustrating the reasons for the declining popularity of Communism in Eastern Europe and the rising influence of evangelical Christianity, Peter referred to a common occurrence in the church of which he was the pastor. His church would frequently have student visitors, young people coming to university in his city, sometimes desperately in need of a place to live. Some of them would be 'loved' into the kingdom, bowled over by the warmth of Christian fellowship and generosity they witnessed in the church. This was because Peter would simply announce the need and ask if any family in the church was willing to take a young university student into their home for a while. These young students never failed to be amazed by the enthusiastic response of church members. This experience often became the crucial breakthrough event, the starting point in a journey to faith. One young communist convert captured the response aptly when he said, 'We have heard the ideals of an egalitarian society described and publicized since we were children, but we saw them practised for the first time in the church!'

The church's sense of community comes not from a man-made utopian ideology of a classless society, but from the experience members share of being incorporated into the family of God through the Holy Spirit. In the opening words of his first epistle, John describes this experience as the natural outcome of a positive response to the proclamation of the gospel of Christ:

> That which was from the beginning, which we have heard, which we have seen with our eyes, which we have looked at and our hands have touched – this we proclaim concerning the Word of life . . . We proclaim to you what we have seen and heard, so that you also may have fellowship with us. And our fellowship is with the Father and with his Son, Jesus Christ. (1 John 1:1, 3)

In all of these images the role of the Spirit is crucial to the being and inner life of the church: in describing the church's basic identity as the community of those among whom God dwells by his Spirit; in emphasizing the essential character of the church as the mystical Body of Christ, an organic extension of his life and mission on earth; in defining the church's membership in terms of God's family comprising all those who share *koinōnia*, a common life in the Spirit. As observed earlier, however, the inner life of the church does overflow into the church's reason for being, its mission in the world.

The church's functions as the community of the Spirit

What is the church doing in the world? is a question Christians and unbelievers alike frequently ask in some form or other. We have already observed that the church derives its essential identity from the Spirit's indwelling presence and members' participation in the *koinōnia*, or common life, of the Spirit. We turn now to a description of four aspects of the Spirit's work in enabling the church to be the church. We look at three of these in this chapter and the fourth in the following chapter.

The Spirit inspires the church in worship

Worship is at the heart of the universe – at the heart of the original creation. Consider the psalmist's exhortation to all of creation to offer exuberant worship to God:

Let the heavens rejoice, let the earth be glad;
>   let the sea resound, and all that is in it;
>   let the fields be jubilant, and everything in them.
Then all the trees of the forest will sing for joy;
>   they will sing before the Lord, for he comes,
>   he comes to judge the earth. . . .

Let the rivers clap their hands,
>   let the mountains sing together for joy.
(Pss 96:11–13; 98:8)

That human beings have been created for worship is a fact that can be observed universally. This human urge to worship finds diverse expression: primeval man's presentation of food or a sacrificial offering to propitiate the natural elements; the Hindu sage whose austere rituals include walking on hot coals or driving sharp metal implements through portions of his flesh; the Shia Muslim whose devotion to Allah leads him to rigorous ritual self-fagellation and severe physical mortification during the period of Moharram; the modern agnostic's careful preservation of his car, yacht, mansion or other symbols of his success and status; the young fan's hysterical adulation of a pop-music or Hollywood celebrity.

When Paul declares that God's ultimate purpose for his children is that we might live for 'the praise of his glory' (Eph. 1:12, 14; cf. 1:6), he clearly underlines the centrality of worship for God's new creation, the church. God's glory is the essence of his nature, the radiance of his splendour, the demonstration of his power – the expression of all he is. The universe exists to show God's glory and for his pleasure. Worship is the only appropriate human response to God's magnificence, as men and women find ultimate fulfilment in and devote their lives to giving God the honour, pleasure and glory due to him. Bringing joy and delight to the heart of God becomes their supreme obsession in life.

The New Testament church was first of all a worshipping community, and the presence of the Holy Spirit was crucial to their worship. In his letter to the Philippians, one of the marks of true believers Paul lists, while defending the truth of the gospel against the legalistic heretics, is that 'we . . . worship by the Spirit of God' (Phil. 3:3). This is in distinct continuity with Jesus' own teaching: in his encounter with the Samaritan woman, he made plain that true worshippers seeking to please the heart of God the Father must worship the Father 'in Spirit and in truth' (John 4:23–24). God thus accepts and approves of worship that is Spirit-directed and in accordance with the truth concerning his nature. What is the kind of worship that pleases God and what is the Spirit's role in facilitating it?

Paul's instructions on worship in 1 Corinthians 14 make it clear that there is much room for freedom in worship, but everything must be done in a peaceful and orderly way (1 Cor. 14:33, 40). Between these two poles of 'freedom' and 'order', Spirit-inspired worship finds expression in a variety of ways. For instance, while liturgical churches follow prescribed orders of worship, free or charismatic churches tend to be more spontaneous in their worship styles. This is especially evident in several majority-world contexts, where the church bells and pipe organ of the older churches exist alongside traditional cultural chants and tribal dance forms, as well as electric guitars and contemporary Western tunes. There need not be any conflict between freedom and order in worship if the same Holy Spirit orchestrates both.

Worship involves two basic kinds of activities that take place between God and the community of his people. One of these is emphasized in Paul's exhortation to believers at Ephesus to

> be filled with the Spirit. Speak to one another with psalms, hymns and spiritual songs. Sing and make music in your heart to the Lord, always giving thanks to God the Father for everything, in the name of our Lord Jesus Christ. (Eph. 5:18–20)

Spirit-led praise, song and prayer are thus directed towards God. But then God speaks to his people through many forms of Spirit-inspired speech, including biblical preaching, teaching and spontaneous prophetic utterances.

'Grant that by the power of the Holy Spirit, these gifts of bread and wine may be to us his body and blood . . .' Some form of this prayer, either liturgically or spontaneously expressed, accompanies the celebration of the Lord's Supper in most churches. This clearly illustrates the importance of the Spirit's role in making the ordinance of Holy Communion meaningful to believers. Just as Jesus comes and speaks to us every time the Word of God is read and preached in the power of the Spirit, so also the Spirit's work in the administering of the Communion makes it a celebration of the presence of the risen Lord. Christian worship is at its richest and best when order and freedom are blended in appropriate measure: when believers sing and praise joyfully, pray fervently, the Bible is read and preached responsibly and the Communion is shared reverently.

The Spirit leads the church to holiness

In the New Testament, the people of God are frequently referred to as 'saints', God's *holy* people. The word *holy* conjures up a wide range of pictures in the minds of people. We think of saints as *holy*, and priests perhaps, and certain designated shrines or places of pilgrimage. Gurus or sadhus in India are undoubtedly among the most diverse class of *holy* men and women in the world, from flamboyant, multi-millionaire 'jet set' yogis who help sustain the multi-billion-dollar global yoga industry, to the eccentric hermits whose rigorous, and occasionally bizarre, ascetic practices create dread and terror among common people. Consequently, although a sense of the *holy* may be found in all of the world's living religions, and frequently pervades all of life in Eastern religions, the concept of holiness is associated closely with superstitious rites and esoteric mystical practices. Holiness thus more often has a 'magical' connotation, having to do with sacred places and objects and the ritual purity of people.

One of the hottest news items in the Indian media during April 2007 was the wedding preparations of two film stars, Aishwarya Rai and Abhishek Bacchan, one a former Miss World and the other the scion of one of the biggest names in the Bollywood film industry, Amitabh Bacchan. The weeks leading up to the wedding saw various members of the family undertake pilgrimages to a number of sacred temples and the invoking of blessing not just from temple deities, but also the priests and holy men at different venues. Astrologers were consulted to confirm whether the gods would be pleased with the alliance and to determine auspicious dates and times. The distribution of the wedding invitations, the colour of the bride's attire, the precise hour when the nuptials were to be concluded – every single detail had to be vetted by a 'holy' person (priest or astrologer) and thus was shot through with a sense of the 'holy'.

How does this sense of the *holy* relate to Peter's declaration when he recalls the words of Yahweh in calling God's people to 'Be holy, for I am holy' (1 Pet. 1:16; cf. Lev. 19:2), and then reminds them of their essential identity and the purpose of their calling: 'But you are a chosen generation . . . a holy nation . . .' (1 Pet. 2:9)? Clearly, the big difference is that the biblical idea of holiness has ethical purity at its core. Thus God's insistence on Israel's holiness comes originally in the context of his detailed moral and ethical instructions to them (Lev. 19:2; 20:7), prominent among these being the demand for sexual purity, consideration towards the poor, honesty, integrity and social justice.

Likewise, Peter's call to holiness exhorts believers to moral purity and ethical living commensurate with their claim of possessing a close relationship to God. This is, of course, only illustrative of the ethical imperative we find in all of the New Testament epistles, where positive teaching or doctrinal correction to believers is always accompanied by exhortation for them to live lives worthy of their claims and calling as children of God.

Holy living is not, however, simply the result of human effort or striving. For, the same Holy Spirit active in God's gracious act of regeneration is responsible for producing the righteousness of God in the lives of believers (Gal. 3:3–5; 5:16–23). The Holy Spirit's presence within the people of God makes them *holy*, gives them identity as the *holy* people of God and effects their moral transformation expressed in ethical righteousness, so they begin to live as the people of God. Life in the Spirit is thus governed not by rules, but by the renewal of the mind through the wisdom and insight the Spirit gives (Rom. 12:1–2; Eph. 1:17; Col. 1:9). The Spirit's role is crucial in that only through his empowering presence can the community of God's people live out ethical behaviour that reflects the character of God to the world.

The people of God are thus expected to exhibit transformed behaviour, to live *holy* lives different from those outside the redeemed community, who do not share in the life of the Holy Spirit. The Spirit enables God's people to abstain from sin and serve God in the newness of life in the Spirit (Rom. 6:1–18; 8:12–13). Believers are thus exhorted to 'walk in the Spirit'/'live by the Spirit' or to behave in accordance with the Spirit (Gal. 5:25), producing virtues in the lives of believers that Paul refers to as the 'fruit of the Spirit': love, joy, peace, patience, kindness, goodness, faithfulness, gentleness and self-control (Gal. 5:22–23).

Thus the idea of 'sanctification' in the New Testament goes beyond the common religious sense (also found in the Old Testament) of a ritual dedication or separation to a call to a life energized by the Holy Spirit that results in *holy*, ethical living as the people of God in the world. In one of Paul's earliest exhortations that captures the essence of New Testament teaching in this regard, he writes:

> It is God's will that you should be sanctified: that you should avoid sexual immorality; that each of you should learn to control his own body in a way that is holy and honourable, not in passionate lust like the heathen, who do not know God; and that in this matter no-one should wrong his brother or take advantage of him. The Lord will

punish men for all such sins, as we have already told you and warned you. For God did not call us to be impure, but to live a holy life. Therefore, he who rejects this instruction does not reject man but God, who gives you his Holy Spirit. (1 Thess. 4:3–8)

The biblical conception of holiness is thus not legalistic and joyless, but radiant and infectious. The Spirit's indwelling does not make us world-denying ascetics or religious eccentrics. Rather, the indwelling power of the Holy Spirit reproduces the lifestyle of Jesus within the community of God's people, observed in the quality of their relationships with one another (Fee 1994: 881). The Spirit seeks to make us spiritually healthy people, living in right relationship to God and to one another, so that we grow into wholeness in body, mind, emotions and actions. The end purpose is so that as we 'become blameless and pure, children of God without fault in a crooked and depraved generation' our lives will shine 'like stars in the universe' and bring glory to our Father in heaven (Phil. 2:15–16; Matt. 5:16).

The Spirit equips the church for ministry

'Why are you doing all this for us?' I looked at the intense expression of the burly and normally intimidating figure who addressed this question to me in sheer disbelief. I had arrived in this north Indian town a few months earlier with the intention of planting a church. One of the families I had been introduced to comprised an elderly couple and three sons, two of whom were married and, in typical Indian tradition, lived together in a large home, enjoying considerable status and influence in their community. The friend who had introduced me had cautioned me about the eldest son. The family had been nominally Christian, but a few years earlier, the only daughter had fallen seriously ill and, despite the best efforts of doctors and fervent prayers of family and friends, had died at the tender age of sixteen. The family was devastated and could not understand how a loving God could have snatched away the one treasured flower in their home. Although the entire family was overwhelmed with grief, the eldest brother was most deeply affected. His heartache quickly hardened into deep depression and bitter antagonism towards God, the Bible and everything to do with the church. More than once he had turned violent against pastors who had visited him and tried to read the Scriptures or pray with him. On an earlier social call I had been advised not even to carry a Bible, for he had been known to wave a gun at anyone who entered his house with a Bible in hand. I complied and survived the elder brother's hostile glare from the doorway.

Two days earlier two friends and I had received a distress call in the middle of the night to minister to the aged father in the fading minutes of his life. Even as he breathed his last the family simply went to pieces over the loss of their father. In the absence of any professional undertakers, my friends and I spontaneously took responsibility for all subsequent practical arrangements. We bathed and dressed the body, contacted relatives and friends, helped clean the house, and conducted the funeral service and interment the next day. A day later I received a summons and was ushered into the presence of the elder brother to hear him speak for the first time. Before I could respond to his question, he turned his head away and with his head in his hands began to sob uncontrollably. At first I thought his tears were due to the pain of bereavement, and undoubtedly his deep sense of loss had contributed to his emotional fragility, but the words were unmistakable: 'We have been so angry against God and treated you all so badly, yet you are doing all this for us . . . why? Why do you serve us like this? Why does God still care about us?'

God gave us the opportunity to explain that we had merely shared with this family in their time of need the grace we had received in the form of gifts the Holy Spirit bestows, so God's people can serve one another. Peter thus makes the source, nature and purpose of spiritual gifts unmistakably clear when he says:

> Each one should use whatever gift he has received to serve others, faithfully administering God's grace in its various forms. If anyone speaks, he should do it as one speaking the very words of God. If anyone serves, he should do it with the strength God provides, so that in all things God may be praised through Jesus Christ. To him be the glory and the power for ever and ever. Amen. (1 Pet. 4:10–11)

Spiritual gifts are special abilities given by the Spirit to every believer for the building up of the church, the body of Christ. A number of New Testament passages deal with the subject of spiritual gifts, and all emphasize that every believer has been endowed with some spiritual gift(s) (Rom. 12:3–8; 1 Cor. 12:4–11; Eph. 4:7–16). In 1 Corinthians 12:4–6, Paul uses three words to designate spiritual gifts, each of which throws light on an important aspect of their nature. *Charisma* (gift) points to God's grace as the source of the gifts: they are not something we earn or work for, but are given freely and graciously by God. *Diakonia* (service) emphasizes the purpose of the gifts:

they are bestowed upon the church as a stewardship to be used for ministry or service towards the building up of the church. *Energēma* (working) describes the effect of the gift's employment: it results in someone being helped and the church being built up.

The church is the one institution in society that exists not for itself but to serve God's purpose in the world. The New Testament clearly teaches that ministry is the privilege and responsibility of all God's people, not just a special class of professional ministry or 'clergy'. All believers have direct access to God, partake of the Holy Spirit and have been bestowed with spiritual gifts. While all spiritual gifts have the same Holy Spirit as their source, not all believers have the same gifts: the Spirit distributes gifts sovereignly as he chooses. There is thus no room for jealousy, feelings of superiority or competitiveness in the exercise of gifts. The church's ministry is, however, integrally and organically related to the spiritual gifts of its members and their willingness to exercise their gifts. A simple if imperfect analogy of the relationship between gift and ministry is that between a car's engine and steering wheel: the engine supplies the power, but the steering wheel is what provides direction to and creative use of the engine's power. The church's ministry is thus directly dependent upon the bestowal and distribution of spiritual gifts, and the gifts are given in order to energize and fuel the church's ministry.

The New Testament, with variation and repetition, lists close to twenty spiritual gifts in four epistles (Rom. 12; 1 Cor. 12; Eph. 4; 1 Pet. 4). Some are easy to relate to, such as teaching, giving, mercy, leadership and administration; others, such as tongues, prophecy, healing and discernment, are supernatural and more spectacular in nature. Then there are other gifts, such as hospitality, celibacy, intercession and exorcism, either mentioned specifically or intimated elsewhere in the New Testament. There is, however, no evidence that the various listings in the New Testament are intended to be systematic or exhaustive. There have also been various attempts to categorize or classify the gifts. The only categorization that may have some basis in Scripture is the differentiation Paul seems to make between *people* who are Christ's gifts to the church (apostles, prophets, pastors, teachers and evangelists) and *activities* that are the result of the Spirit's empowerment of believers (such as tongues, teaching, healing, giving and prophecy). Church traditions that believe in an ordained leadership would regard the gifts as belonging to the former category.

Spiritual gifts are defined fairly broadly in the New Testament, and include both the more dramatic 'supernatural' signs as well as the less spectacular 'natural' gifts that are also essential to the life of the church. The ultimate purpose of all the gifts, however, is to help the community of God's people to serve one another more effectively and thus grow into maturity, and, as a result, draw unbelievers to Christ. The church will grow as every believer discovers, uses and develops his or her spiritual gift. In continuing the ministry of Jesus on the earth, God's people are called to serve not only one another but the world outside as well.

Marks of the Spirit: signs of the kingdom in the church

The church exists in the world not for its own sake but to announce the kingdom of God and demonstrate its reality. The present world system is out of tune with the values of the kingdom, and constantly puts pressure on God's people to conform to its standards. The church is called to be *in* the world and yet not *of* the world. God's people are called to be different, to live a counter-cultural lifestyle that reflects kingdom values. The Holy Spirit's principal function in the church today is to authenticate the church's claim that the kingdom has arrived, and he does so by reproducing the values and virtues of the kingdom, such as righteousness, peace, love, joy, healing and reconciliation. These marks of the Spirit's presence and power in the church are thus also signs of the kingdom.

The Holy Spirit enables the church to fulfil its role as a *sign* (providing evidence that the kingdom has already arrived in the first coming of Christ), and a *signpost* (pointing to the future coming of the kingdom in fullness at the second coming of Christ). History bears eloquent testimony to the fact that the church frequently fails to evidence the reality of the kingdom through its life and witness. However, whenever God's people have returned to him in repentance, the breath of his Spirit has renewed the church, restoring it to its original biblical calling and purpose.

9

Keeping in Step with the Spirit

The Spirit in the World

I am not normally an early riser, but this morning I was up unusually early and wound my way to the back of our 21-acre campus as the first rays of the sun peeped over the horizon. (I like to walk as I pray: it helps me concentrate and at the same time get a little exercise.) I had barely begun to pour my heart out in prayer when I became aware of the earliest sounds of a waking world: the familiar music of birds singing, the chickens and cows from the farm next door, the sound of the occasional motor car and, in the midst of this cacophony of sounds, the sounds of religious devotion. First the drums, cymbals and chants from the temple in the adjoining village; then the distant strains of the Muslim maulvi's rising cry from the mosque, calling people to pray; and finally, the sounds of worship from our own chapel as early risers gathered for a brief time of prayer. Questions I had struggled with from my earliest years as a believer came back to me with renewed vigour:

- Is the Spirit present only here on our campus and within the sacred precincts of our chapel?
- Is he active only within the believing community where Jesus is glorified, the triune God is worshipped and the Bible is believed, taught and practised?
- Does the all-powerful, all-knowing, ever-present Holy Spirit ignore completely the sincere cries of Hindu devotees and Muslim worshippers?
- Do they experience nothing of the Spirit whatsoever?

For me, this was not just a theoretical issue but a burning existential question. Most of my neighbours and friends throughout my childhood were not Christians, and after I came to Christ I wondered about their future every time I heard that those without Christ would go to hell. I spent much of my time in the first few years of my ministry on the streets and crowded slums of one of the most densely populated cities in the world, Mumbai. On the way home in a crowded local train, after spending several hours preaching and witnessing on the streets, I would wonder about the tens of thousands who streamed in and out at every station: *Could the Spirit be at work in any of their hearts?* Through marriage, two of my close family members have come from other faiths: one, a devout Muslim; the other, Zoroastrian. One has since come to faith in Christ and is a radiant believer, but the other remains resistant.

Is the Spirit at work among people of other faiths? Some Christians find it easy to say a glib, unqualified 'No' to this question, since the Holy Spirit's presence and activity is Christ-centred and is consequent upon the objective revelation and reconciliation in Jesus Christ. Those who say a simple 'Yes' do not differentiate between the Holy Spirit and the general immanence of God, and consequently have no problem conceding that the Spirit is present and at work everywhere in the same way he is among the believing community. Is it possible to affirm the Christ-centred presence and activity of the Spirit while recognizing his work in the world in the midst of people of other faiths and no faith? In chapter 3 we saw the Bible teaches that the Spirit is present and active everywhere in creation. The challenge is to be able to recognize where he is at work in the midst of a fallen world marred by sin. The simple test is *Christ* – wherever Christ is worshipped, his lordship acknowledged, his word celebrated, his will affirmed and his kingdom purpose advanced, the Holy Spirit must be at work. The Spirit's movement in the world has essentially two directions: he (1) equips the church for mission in the world, and (2) draws the world to Christ and his kingdom.

The Spirit empowers the church for mission

One could attempt to define the mission of the church in various ways. One way is to focus on the life and ministry of Jesus, and to view the church's mission as a continuation of Jesus' mission. The basis for this is clearly set forth in the Fourth Gospel in at least two places: 'As you sent me into the world, I have sent them into the world'; and again, 'As the Father has sent me, I am sending you' (John 17:18; 20:21). The word 'as' here has crucial significance, since it suggests that the way the Father sent the Son determines the way Jesus sends the church (Newbigin 1987: 23).

The Gospels clearly indicate that Jesus' mission on earth was inseparably connected to the kingdom of God. At the outset of his mission, 'Jesus went into Galilee, proclaiming the good news of God. "The time has come," he said. "The kingdom of God is near. Repent and believe the good news!" ' (Mark 1:14–15). This continued to be the central theme of his ministry all through his earthly life: his parables concerned the kingdom, his signs witnessed to the arrival of the kingdom and his teaching focused on the virtues and values of the kingdom.

It is thus impossible to separate the kingdom of God from the person of Jesus, for it is in the life and ministry of Christ that the kingdom of God has become a present reality. In Christ, God has acted decisively to fulfil his redemptive purpose: the kingdom of God has already broken into history and is present among men and women in great power in the person of Jesus. Although the new age has been inaugurated in Christ, the consummation of the new age still remains in the future. The kingdom of God is, consequently, both a present reality and a promise that awaits future fulfilment. Jesus' mission thus consisted essentially in making known and manifesting the reality of the kingdom of God (Padilla 1985: 186–189).

The works of Jesus were closely linked to his words. For instance, when the Pharisees accused him of casting out demons by Satan's authority, Jesus countered their charge with the claim that his acts of power were evidence that the kingdom of God had arrived in his person, and demonstrated the reality of the kingdom (Matt. 12:24–28). The words and works of Jesus were, however, directed towards a clear end: extending the kingdom rule of God in the hearts of people. The kingdom of God is thus central to a biblical understanding of mission, and mission must be church-centred. It is to the community of his followers (the church) that Christ entrusts the completion of his mission and the commission to make disciples of all nations (Matt. 28:18–20; Acts 1:8).

The Holy Spirit played a crucial role in every aspect of the kingdom mission of Jesus. At Pentecost the Spirit came on the early church in power so Jesus' mission could be advanced and completed. There is thus an indissoluble relationship between Pentecost and the missionary witness of the church. The witness of the church began at Pentecost, and in the power of the Pentecostal Spirit this witness continues to be carried forward (Boer 1975: 110).

Jesus' declaration that the kingdom of God had arrived in his person is clearly set against the backdrop of a real but invisible conflict between two kingdoms: the kingdom of God and the kingdom of this world or the ruler/prince of this world, Satan (Matt. 12:26, 28). The church of Jesus Christ continues to be engaged in constant spiritual warfare with the principalities and powers of evil in the world (Eph. 6:11–12), but the gospel is the good news of Jesus Christ's victory over the powers of evil (Col. 2:15; Heb. 2:14–15). The role of the Holy Spirit in mission is thus critical in the light of this conflict between the kingdom of God and the powers of evil. The Holy Spirit provides the people of God with the power required for spiritual resistance against the idolatrous, enslaving and destructive activity of the powers of evil (Luke 10:18–19; 24:48–49; Acts 1:8) The empowerment of the Holy Spirit thus impacts every aspect of the church's mission.

Verbal witness

Jesus launched his ministry when he stood up and read from the scroll of Isaiah,

> The Spirit of the Lord is on me,
>> because he has anointed me
>> to *preach* good news to the poor.
> He has sent me to *proclaim* freedom for the prisoners
>> and recovery of sight for the blind,
> to release the oppressed,
>> to *proclaim* the year of the Lord's favour.
> (Luke 4:18–19; my italics)

Jesus' declaration captures the prophetic dimension of mission: the Spirit empowers God's people to *proclaim* or *preach*. This is the verbal witness to the arrival of the kingdom. Something new has happened: the reign of God has come near, and this fact must be announced. But, as Paul points out, 'The god of this age has blinded the minds of unbelievers, so that they cannot see the light of the gospel . . .' (2 Cor. 4:4). The Spirit anoints representatives of the kingdom and empowers them to proclaim that the kingdom has arrived in Christ (Luke 4:18; Acts 4:29, 31).

Works of power and loving service

The kingdom must not only be announced; its reality must be demonstrated 'in power'. Paul declares to the Corinthian Christians that 'My message and my preaching were not with wise and persuasive words, but with a demonstration of the Spirit's power, so that your faith might . . . rest . . . on God's power' (1 Cor. 2:4–5). A feature of the period of the end (between the first and second coming of Jesus) is the presence of the Spirit in the church. The book of Acts is filled with dramatic instances of what we sometimes refer to as 'power encounters': supernatural healings, exorcisms and other miraculous signs. However, the radical nature of the love, sharing of life (*koinōnia*) and mutual service experienced by the early church also demonstrated in power the reality of the kingdom's presence in their midst (Acts 3:6–10; 5:12–16; 2:42–47; 4:32–37).

This includes what is sometimes referred to as the church's 'social witness'. Powerful forces in the world work against the New Testament vision of a single new humanity in Christ. Race, caste, greed, economic exploitation, social oppression and injustice resist the kingdom forces of change, and, on the other hand, sow discord and strife where peace and harmony prevail. Believers fall short of their calling and compromise their true identity when they permit these evil forces to control and condition behaviour in the church. Only by the power of the Spirit is the church able to resist these forces of evil that hold sway in society, and fulfil her function as 'sign' or agent of God's kingdom in the world. Thus the Spirit's personal presence enables the church to demonstrate the reality of the kingdom in its works of power and loving service.

Making disciples

According to Matthew's Gospel, Jesus' last command before his ascension was to 'Go and *make disciples* of all nations . . .' (Matt. 28:19; my italics). We observe how the apostles fulfilled Jesus' instructions concerning this in the book of Acts as they invited both Jews and Gentiles to turn from their sins and put their faith in Christ. For instance, we read in Acts 2:41, 'Those who accepted his message were baptized, and about three thousand were added to their number that day,' and shortly after in 4:4 that 'many who heard the message believed, and the number of men grew to about five thousand'.

The task of making disciples, which commenced first in Jerusalem, involved planting new communities of believers among both Jews and Gentiles in other towns and cities. Thus the believing community, the church, continued to grow first in Jerusalem, then in Judea and Samaria, and spread throughout Palestine and Asia Minor, eventually crossing the Mediterranean to the shores of Europe. Everywhere the earliest missionaries went they preached Christ and him crucified, resulting in many turning to Christ and becoming his disciples. The Holy Spirit thus had an important role to play not only in empowered proclamation and demonstration of the kingdom's reality, but in extending the rule of God in the hearts of those who accepted Christ's lordship and became his followers.

Those without Christ were regarded as 'dead in transgressions and sins' (Eph. 2:1; Rom. 5:12). Becoming a disciple of Christ thus entails a radical work of the Holy Spirit based on Christ's atoning death, by which those who trust in him have their sins forgiven and partake of eternal life (1 Pet. 2:24; 2 Cor. 5:21). Salvation is thus a 'power encounter', where the Holy Spirit *convicts* (John 16:8–10) and then *regenerates*, emplanting the divine nature within the heart of the repentant sinner (John 1:13; 3:3–8; 1 Pet. 1:23). The Spirit works powerfully in the heart of disciples, releasing them from bondage to sin and Satan and creating new life within (2 Cor. 5:17; Eph. 2:5, 6; 1 Pet. 1:3).

As the disciple continues to grow in her new relationship with Christ through prayer, diligent study of God's Word and commitment to the fellowship of local believers, the signs of spiritual maturity are seen as the new nature begins to affect every aspect of her personality and lifestyle. Thus, just as sin has affected every aspect of a person's being, the benefits of Christ's death have a bearing on every aspect of the human personality. While the new life we receive in Christ makes us primarily new creatures within through the life of the Spirit, this life must overflow and affect physical, mental and emotional health and wholeness, restoring human dignity and divine likeness lost through the fall.

Spiritual warfare

An essential aspect of the missionary enterprise where the Spirit plays a crucial role is prayer. Jesus taught his disciples to pray for the coming of the kingdom:

> Your kingdom come,
> your will be done
>   on earth as it is in heaven.
> (Matt. 6:10)

Prayer is thus sometimes described as 'the cry of the kingdom'. Some see a cosmic spiritual warfare at the root of the missionary enterprise, where the kingdom of God through the church is pitted against the principalities and powers under the control of 'the prince of this world' (John 12:31; Eph. 6:12;

Dan. 10). Although God is sovereign and in control of the affairs of the universe, he has entrusted us with an essential key for seeing his kingdom established on earth. The Holy Spirit has a vital role in advancing the kingdom mission of Christ as he equips, empowers and energizes the church to confront the cosmic forces of evil through prayer and intercession. This is an area of New Testament teaching that often tends to be neglected by the church, and is in urgent need of recovery (Rom. 8:26–27; Eph. 6:18).

The powers of darkness must be engaged in spiritual combat through intercession at every level. Their influence in the lives of individuals, in the church and in social and political structures must all likewise be resisted and the victory of Christ enforced in the power of the Spirit (1 Tim. 2:1–2; 1 Thess. 5:17; Mark 9:29; Eph. 6:19–20; Col. 4:12). Consequently, through prayer and intercession in the Spirit 'the kingdom of heaven has been forcefully advancing', and the kingdom mission of Christ advances as the church is 'forceful' in laying hold of it in prayer (Matt. 11:12).

The Spirit draws the world to Christ

The images have been etched in our minds and will remain there perhaps for ever. Thousands of miles away in our home in Bangalore, India, students crowded our living room, all eyes glued to the television screen as, numb with shock, we watched the towers of the World Trade Center come crumbling down before our eyes. What has come to be known as '9/11' was a watershed not just in American history but is an episode in modern times that has permanently impacted the way we live. The images of grief and devastation will endure for a long while: the senseless loss of lives, the faces of children who became orphans overnight, rescue workers trying their best to pick up the pieces of broken lives, grim world leaders trying to impart comfort, strength and encouragement to people with shattered worlds.

But perhaps the most significant insight that emerged when the shock waves had subsided was the frightening realization that religion had returned as a major factor in global conflict. Five years earlier, in his *The Clash of Civilizations and the Remaking of World Order*, Samuel Huntington had predicted that conflicts between civilizations would dominate the future of world politics. September 11 clearly marked the fulfilment of this prophecy, but with religious ideology occupying centre stage. The upsurge of fundamentalism in all religions has consequently become a matter of great concern, since fundamentalist ideology in any religion appears to generate hatred, suspicion and fear in its followers towards other religions. Recent works documenting the rise of religious terrorism have pointed out the close connection between religious fundamentalism and terrorist violence, highlighting the frequently chilling fanaticism of true believers within all of the world's major traditions, including Christianity, Islam, Hinduism, Judaism, Buddhism and Sikhism. Many see the real enemy as neither 'terrorism' per se, nor even Islamic fanaticism, but religious fundamentalism.

For instance, Thomas Friedman, author of the best-seller *The Lexus and the Olive Tree*, is one who sees the real enemy as religious totalitarianism: 'a view of the world that my faith must reign supreme and can be affirmed and held passionately only if all others are negated'. Friedman sees the only hope for future global peace and social harmony in pluralism: 'an ideology that embraces religious diversity and the idea that my faith can be nurtured without claiming exclusive truth . . . a multilingual view of God – a notion that God is not exhausted by just one religious path' (Friedman 2001).

While religious plurality has been an integral part of life within the human community since time immemorial, in today's world it has become a burning issue, with critical existential and sociopolitical consequences. Committed Christians thus find themselves on the defensive, under compulsion to revisit difficult questions relating to our attitude to the diverse faiths of our neighbours:

- What is distinctive about the Christian message in a world of many faiths?
- If Christ is my Saviour, does that imply he is the only Saviour?
- If Christ is the only way to God, what about the millions of non Jewish people who lived prior to his coming?
- If every religion claims to be the only true one and sees its mission as converting those of other faiths, will it not intensify religious bigotry, fanaticism and communal strife?

The issue is not as novel as some contemporary treatments seem to imply when they suggest that the modern experience of religious plurality has compelled the church to rethink its response to non-Christian religious experience. The fact is, however, that the intrinsic missionary nature of the Christian faith, arising from its original constituting fact (the Christ-event and claims of decisiveness and universality integral to it) has forced the church to address this since the earliest stages of its contact with the nonChristian world.

Christian responses to this issue generally converge around two poles. At one extreme are those who, in accordance with the spirit of the times feel that any group claiming to have received unique and privileged knowledge or experience of the divine is both misled and arrogant. Tradition-specific approaches must be abandoned in favour of pluralist approaches, since all religions, more or less, lead to the same divine reality. Hence any claims of finality or decisiveness of Christ must be abandoned in the interests of preserving religious and social harmony.

In reacting to this, conservative Christians have tended to gravitate to the other extreme, affirming strongly that only one single revelation or religion is true, *Christianity*, and all other revelations or religions are false. Revelation is restricted exclusively to one particular tradition, and salvation to one particular community, with the rest of humankind either left out of account or explicitly excluded from the sphere of salvation. In our concern to preserve the uniqueness of Christ, evangelical Christians thus frequently see no alternative but to dismiss the fact and empirical data of other religions without fair scrutiny.

Many see a solution to this dilemma in discerning the work of the Holy Spirit outside the church among people of other faiths and no faith. Those seeking to ascribe some value to nonChristian religious experience, however, sometimes stray from biblical faith when they try to speak of the Spirit or of the Trinity apart from the Jesus of history. The Holy Spirit is not just any spirit and must not be confused either with the human spirit or with an impersonal monist conception of spirit such as Brahman in Hinduism. The Holy Spirit is the Spirit *of Christ*, and the Christian concept of the Trinity is derived from the historical fact of the incarnation. The Holy Spirit is not the only spirit at work in the world – there are other 'spirits' in the world.

John offers the following words of caution in his first epistle: 'This is how you can recognize the Spirit of God: Every spirit that acknowledges that Jesus Christ has come in the flesh is from God, but every spirit that does not acknowledge Jesus is not from God' (1 John 4:2–3). There is, thus, a need for spiritual discernment to distinguish between authentic and counterfeit manifestations of the Holy Spirit's presence, between what is legitimately the activity of the Spirit of Christ and what is not.

Our study of the work of the Holy Spirit thus far has, however, equipped us with important biblical criteria for recognizing the presence and activity of the Spirit. Jesus promised that the Spirit *of truth* would guide us into all truth and that he would *testify* about and *bring glory* to Jesus (John 15:26;

16:13–14). This provides us with helpful means for identifying where and how the Spirit is at work outside the church, and further for employing these for building bridges between Christ and the religious experience of people of other faiths. We are able to cooperate with the Spirit as he seeks to draw them to faith in Christ.

In seeking to affirm the finality of Christ, it is thus unhelpful to discount a priori any pointers whatsoever to redemptive truths in other religious traditions. Dewi Hughes's sweeping dismissal of Hinduism is a good illustration:

> It may be possible to argue that there is a longing in the heart of everyone for the true God who comes in Jesus, but that there is no evidence of such a longing in the religion which has developed in India. In the experience of missionaries the opposite is true – Hindu religion is the greatest hindrance to the acceptance of Jesus as the true and final revelation of God. (Hughes 1996: 228–229)

Hughes's categorical verdict simply does not fit with the empirical facts. As far back as the eighteenth century, the German missionary Ziegenbalg's careful study of the Hindu religious texts led him to write home concerning 'a small light of the gospel' he observed within Hinduism. Subsequently, during the nineteenth and early twentieth century an impressive number of informed missionaries recognized distinct anticipations of Christ within Hinduism. More importantly, the experience of converts from Hinduism in India corroborates this as well. The celebrated nineteenth-century scholar-apologist K. M. Banerjea's study of the Hindu scriptures, the Vedas, in the light of his Christian experience convinced him that the atoning sacrifice of Christ was prefigured in the vedic concept of *prajapati*, a primeval cosmic sacrifice for sins. The Hindu convert N. V. Tilak claimed to have come to Christ as a result of the anticipations he saw and experienced in the rich devotional poetry of the Hindu *bhakti* movement.

A commitment to the decisiveness and finality of Christ thus enables us to follow the Spirit in freely pursuing truth, beauty and goodness wherever they may be found. If and when we find them in the midst of non-Christian religions and cultures, we are not afraid to celebrate their existence and use them as 'landing strips' to communicate the gospel of Christ. As the opening illustration in chapter 1 illustrates, this enables us to share our experience of Christ with others as fellow pilgrims on a common quest for a genuine experience of God. This prepares the way for a nonoffensive yet effective approach in communicating the gospel to people of other faiths, where we meaningfully engage their religious experiences and use 'redemptive' intimations we discover in their beliefs, experiences and aspirations as points of contact in sharing the gospel.

Not too long ago, some friends and I had the opportunity of visiting the plush ashram or 'monastery' of an extraordinarily popular guru. His popularity had made him a figure of global repute, so he was in great demand in North America and other parts of the Western world, even earning him an invitation to address a forum of the United Nations. The setting was plush and impressive, and the atmosphere among the several hundred devotees gathered in the assembly hall for the evening meditation was charged. The guru's flowing locks of hair, beard and spotless white robe would elicit an inevitable comparison with an artist's impression of Christ, and as he began to speak, the congregation listened in rapt attention.

At the end of the discourse we had the good fortune of being granted a private audience. My pastor friend and I had led a funeral service earlier that afternoon and could not resist asking the question 'Jesus offers his followers eternal life beyond the grave based on his resurrection from the dead. What hope do you give your thousands of devotees when they depart from this world?' After a brief pause, with a wry smile he gave us a response that left us in stunned disbelief: 'I do not plan my answers ahead of time. I say what the spirit gives me each time . . .' It appeared to me that several of his followers bowed their heads in disappointment or embarrassment at the great guru's answer to such a vital question of life.

Of course, this man has no answer. Christ alone offers real hope beyond the grave, and this man neither knows Christ nor has the Spirit of Christ. Then it came to me. I thought of all the vibrant expressions of devotion I had observed earlier among the devotees as they sang, chanted and danced, listened closely to their guru's discourse, asked questions and literally kissed the ground he walked on, in their desperate hunger for a touch of the divine presence. Could the Spirit be at work in these imperfect but passionate expressions of devotion and deep longing after God? I tend to think so.

My conviction was tested as we made our way out of the guru's inner chamber to the parking lot outside. The lady who escorted us listened intently as we shared briefly about the hope we have in Christ. I believe, like millions of others in our world, she was searching for a genuine experience of God. But not every religious experience is an authentic experience of God. A genuine experience of God involves a life-transforming encounter with the living God through the Spirit as we respond to the testimony of Jesus Christ recorded in the Bible.

The Holy Spirit is in the business of drawing the world to Christ, but where is Christ seen today? The world has a right to look for him in the church, the community of people who claim to be Christ's followers. The church will look like Christ to the extent that the Holy Spirit is allowed to work in the lives of her members. The world witnessed a powerful illustration of this in the wake of a gruesome tragedy that struck an Australian missionary family in India on 23 January 1999. Graham and Gladys Staines had been working in a small village in the state of Orissa in North India for close to four decades, and were greatly loved for their work among leprosy patients. Graham and his two young sons, Philip and Timothy, were brutally killed by fanatical Hindu extremists. The President of India himself led the nation in expressing the deep sense of outrage and shame felt by millions of Indians. The morning after the incident a grief-stricken Gladys Staines was asked for her reaction to the heinous crime and her feelings towards the murderers. She simply and spontaneously said, 'I forgive them.' Through her brokenness and pain a land of one billion people saw the face of Jesus and heard the voice of the Spirit. Those three words became the shortest but most effective sermon India has ever heard, and the message reverberated all over the country long after. The response of the nation was perhaps most suitably captured in the words of Swami Agnivesh, a well-known Hindu religious leader: 'If this is Christianity, we want it in India!'

The Holy Spirit's role is thus indispensable to the church's missionary enterprise. When the Holy Spirit is given his rightful place at the helm of the church's missionary programme, we shall see God's kingdom mission continue to advance in our generation. For the kingdom of God is extended and established, as the prophet of old declared over two thousand years ago, '"Not by might nor by power, but by my Spirit," says the Lord Almighty' (Zech. 4:6).

Lord, thank you for sending the Holy Spirit to be your presence in our lives. Help us to yield our will to yours and to allow the Holy Spirit to change our hearts and purify our lives. May we always be sensitive to the voice of the Holy Spirit drawing us closer to you, we pray in Jesus' name.

Amen.

BIBLIOGRAPHY

Berdyaev, N. (1946), *Spirit and Reality*, London: G. Bles.

Bloesch, D. G. (2000), *The Holy Spirit*, Downers Grove: IVP.

Boer, H. (1975), *Pentecost and Missions*, Grand Rapids: Eerdmans.

Bruner, F. D. (1970), *A Theology of the Holy Spirit: The Pentecostal Experience and the New Testament Witness*, Grand Rapids: Eerdmans.

Burgess, S. M., and E. M. van der Maas (eds.) (2002), *The New International Dictionary of Pentecostal and Charismatic Movements*, Grand Rapids: Zondervan.

Burleigh, J. H. S. (1954), 'The Doctrine of the Holy Spirit in the Latin Fathers', *Scottish Journal of Theology* 7: 113–132.

Chenchiah, P. D., G. V. Job and D. M. Devasahayam et al. (1939), *Rethinking Christianity in India*, Madras: A. N. Sudarisanam.

Dunn, J. D. G. (1970), *Baptism in the Holy Spirit*, London: SCM.

Durasoff, S. (1972), *Bright Wind of the Spirit*, Englewood Cliffs, N. J.: Prentice-Hall.

Erickson, M. J. (1985), *Christian Theology*, vol. 3, Grand Rapids: Baker.

Fee, G. D. (1994), *God's Empowering Presence: The Holy Spirit in the Letters of Paul*, Peabody: Hendrickson.

Fénelon, F. (1997), *Talking with God*, tr. Hal. M. Helms, Brewster, Mass.: Paraclete.

Friedman, T. (2001), 'The Real War', *New York Times*, 27 Nov.

Gaybba, B. (1987), *The Spirit of Love*, London: Geoffrey Chapman.

Glaser, I. (2005), *The Bible and Other Faiths*, Leicester: IVP.

Haroutunian, J. (1974), 'The Church, the Spirit, and the Hands of God', *Journal of Religion* 54: 154–165.

Hughes, D. A. (1996), *Has God Many Names?*, Leicester: Apollos.

Kärkkäinen, V. (1998), *Spiritus ubi vult. spirat: Pneumatology in Roman Catholic–Pentecostal Dialogue (1972–1989)*, Helsinki: Luther Agricola-Society.

Kelsey, M. T. (1972), *Encounter with God: A Theology of Christian Experience*, *Bloomington*, Minn.: Bethany House.

King, U. (ed.) (1994), *Feminist Theology from the Third World: A Reader*, Maryknoll: Orbis.

Lederle, H. I. (1988), *Treasures Old and New: Interpretations of 'Spirit-Baptism' in the Charismatic Renewal Movement*, Peabody: Hendrickson.

Lewis, G. R., and B. A. Demarest (1996), *Integrative Theology*, Grand Rapids: Zondervan.

McDonnell, K. (1985), 'A Trinitarian Theology of the Holy Spirit', *Theological Studies* 46: 191–227.

—— (2003), *The Other Hand of God: The Holy Spirit as the Universal Touch and Goal*, Collegeville, Minn.: Liturgical.

McGrath, A. (1994), *Christian Theology: An Introduction*, Oxford: Blackwell.

Montague, G. T. (1976), *The Holy Spirit: Growth of a Biblical Tradition*, Peabody: Hendrickson.

Naisbitt, J., and P. Aburdene (1990), *Megatrends 2000: Ten New Directions for the 1990s*, New York: William Morrow.

Nanez, R. M. (2005), *Full Gospel, Fractured Minds?*, Grand Rapids: Zondervan.

Newbigin, L. (1987), *Mission in Christ's Way*, Geneva: WCC.

Packer, J. I. (2005), *Keep in Step with the Spirit*, 2nd ed., Grand Rapids: Baker; Leicester: IVP.

Padilla, C. R. (1985), *Mission between the Times*, Grand Rapids: Eerdmans.

Pelikan, J. (ed.) (1957), *Luther's Works*, vol. 22, tr. Martin H.Bertram, St. Louis: Concordia.

Plantinga, C. (1988), 'Trinity', in G. W. Bromiley (ed.), *International Standard Bible Encyclopedia*, Grand Rapids: Eerdmans, 24–27.

Rajghatta, C. (2005), 'Katrina Fails to Wet Granth Sahib', *Times of India*, 8 Sept.

Stott, J. R. W. (1979), *The Message of Ephesians*, Leicester: IVP.

—— (1990), *The Message of Acts*, Leicester: IVP.

Streeter, B. H., and A. J. Appasamy (1987), *The Sadhu: A Study in Mysticism and Practical Religion*, London: Macmillan, 1921; repr. Delhi: Mittal.

Swete, H. B. (1912), *The Holy Spirit: A Study of Christian Teaching in the Age of the Fathers*, London: McMillan.

Taylor, J. V. (1972), *The Go-between God*, London: SCM.

Turner, M. (1998), *The Holy Spirit and Spiritual Gifts*, Peabody: Hendrickson.

Wainwright, A. (1962), *The Trinity in the New Testament*, London: SPCK.

Welch, C. (1953), *The Trinity in Contemporary Theology*, London: SCM.

Wiersbe, W. W. (1978), *Be Mature: James: Growing up in Christ* Wheaton, Ill.: Victor.

Williams, John (1980), *The Holy Spirit: Lord and Life-Giver*, Neptune, N. J.: Loizeaux Brothers.

Williams, J. Rodman (1990), *Renewal Theology: Salvation, the Holy Spirit and Christian Living*, Grand Rapids: Zondervan.

Wright, C. J. H. (2006), *Knowing the Holy Spirit through the Old Testament*, Leicester: IVP.

Langham PARTNERSHIP

Langham Partnership is working to strengthen the church in the majority world. We provide doctoral scholarships for future principals and teachers at majority world seminaries and for those who will take up strategic positions of leadership in the church. We send carefully chosen evangelical books, as gifts or at low cost, to church pastors and to teachers at Bible colleges, and we foster the writing and publishing of Christian literature in many regional languages. We also run training workshops and produce materials to raise the standard of biblical preaching and teaching, and work to develop preaching networks locally. For further information see www.langham.org or email global@langham.org

CPSIA information can be obtained
at www.ICGtesting.com
Printed in the USA
LVHW02s1113170818
587285LV00022BA/2023/P